CAREER IDEAS
for kids who like
ANIMALS AND NATURE

**DIANE LINDSEY REEVES
AND NANCY HEUBECK**

Illustrations by
NANCY BOND

Checkmark Books™
An imprint of Facts On File, Inc.

CAREER IDEAS FOR KIDS WHO LIKE ANIMALS AND NATURE

Checkmark Books
An imprint of Facts On File, Inc.
11 Penn Plaza
New York NY 10001

Library of Congress Cataloging-in-Publication Data

Reeves, Diane Lindsey, 1959–
    Career ideas for kids who like animals and nature / Diane Lindsey
Reeves and Nancy Heubeck : illustrations by Nancy Bond.
      p. cm. — (Career ideas for kids who like)
    Includes bibliographical references.
    Summary: Discusses such animal- and nature-related careers as
animal trainer, arborist, land surveyor, and zoologist, and discusses
how to determine which career might be suitable and how to prepare for it.
    ISBN 0-8160-4097-4 (hardcover). — ISBN 0-8160-4098-2 (pbk.)
    1. Life sciences—Vocational guidance Juvenile literature.
2. Outdoor life—Vocational guidance Juvenile literature.
3. Zoology—Vocational guidance Juvenile literature.   [1. Life
sciences—Vocational guidance. 2. Outdoor life—Vocational guidance.
3. Zoology—Vocational guidance. 4. Vocational guidance.]
    I. Heubeck, Nancy. II. Bond, Nancy, ill. III. Title. IV. Series: Reeves,
Diane Lindsey, 1959–   Career ideas for kids who like.
QH314.R44   2000
570'.23—dc21   99-37735

ACKNOWLEDGMENTS

A million thanks to the people who took the time to share
their career stories and provide photos for this book:

Robert Julian Allen III
Don Blair
Gene Bobbitt
Laura Bourhenne
Douglas Boyer
Peg Brandon
Christine Foster
Mindy Green
Kathy Marmack
Larry Sokolowski
Chichie Tascoe
Mia Tegner
John R. Watts
Dean Wheeler
Phyllis Yoyetewa

Also, special thanks to the design team of Smart Graphics,
Nancy Bond, and Cathy Rincon for bringing the
Career Ideas for Kids series to life with their creative talent.

Finally, much appreciation and admiration is due to
my editor, Nicole Bowen, whose vision and attention
to detail increased the quality of this project in
many wonderful ways.

CONTENTS

You're young. Most of your life is still ahead of you. How are you supposed to know what you want to be when you grow up?

You're right: 10, 11, 12, 13 is a bit young to know exactly what and where and how you're going to do whatever it is you're going to do as an adult. But, it's the perfect time to start making some important discoveries about who you are, what you like to do, and what you do best. It's the ideal time to start thinking about what you *want* to do.

Make a choice! If you get a head start now, you may avoid setbacks and mistakes later on.

When it comes to picking a career, you've basically got two choices.

CHOICE A

Wait until you're in college to start figuring out what you want to do. Even then you still may not decide what's up your alley, so you graduate and jump from job to job still searching for something you really like.

Hey, it could work. It might be fun. Lots of (probably most) people do it this way.

The problem is that if you pick Choice A, you may end up settling for second best. You may miss out on a meaningful education, satisfying work, and the rewards of a focused and well-planned career.

You have another choice to consider.

CHOICE B

Start now figuring out your options and thinking about the things that are most important in your life's work: Serving others? Staying true to your values? Making lots of money? Enjoying your work? Your young years are the perfect time to mess around with different career ideas without messing up your life.

Reading this book is a great idea for kids who choose B. It's a first step toward choosing a career that matches your skills, interests, and lifetime goals. It will help you make a plan for tailoring your junior and high school years to fit your career dreams. To borrow a jingle from the U.S. Army—using this book is a way to discover how to "be all that you can be."

Ready for the challenge of Choice B? If so, read the next section to find out how this book can help start you on your way.

HOW TO USE THIS BOOK

This isn't just a book about interesting careers that other people have. It's a book about interesting careers that you can have.

Of course, it won't do you a bit of good to just read this book. To get the whole shebang, you're going to have to jump in with both feet, roll up your sleeves, put on your thinking cap—whatever it takes—to help you do these three things:

☀ **Discover** what you do best and enjoy the most. (This is the secret ingredient for finding work that's perfect for you.)

- 💡 **Explore** ways to match your interests and abilities with career ideas.
- 💡 **Experiment** with lots of different ideas until you find the ideal career. (It's like trying on all kinds of hats to see which ones fit!)

Use this book as a road map to some exciting career destinations. Here's what to expect in the chapters that follow.

GET IN GEAR!

First stop: self-discovery. These activities will help you uncover important clues about the special traits and abilities that make you *you*. When you are finished you will have developed a personal Skill Set that will help guide you to career ideas in the next chapter.

TAKE A TRIP!

Next stop: exploration. Cruise down the career idea highway and find out about a variety of career ideas that are especially appropriate for people who like animals and nature. Use the Skill Set chart at the beginning of each entry to match your own interests with those required for success on the job.

MAKE A NATURAL DETOUR!

Here's your chance to explore an amazing array of occupations involving animals and nature. Just when you thought you'd seen it all, here come dozens of new ideas to add to the mix. Spice up your career search by learning all you can about some of these exciting opportunities.

DON'T STOP NOW!

Third stop: experimentation. The library, the telephone, a computer, and a mentor—four keys to a successful career planning adventure. Use them well, and before long you'll be on the trail of some hot career ideas.

WHAT'S NEXT?

Make a plan! Chart your course (or at least the next stop) with these career planning road maps. Whether you're moving full steam ahead with a great idea or get slowed down at a yellow light of indecision, these road maps will keep you moving forward toward a great future.

Use a pencil—you're bound to make a detour or two along the way. But, hey, you've got to start somewhere.

HOORAY! YOU DID IT!

Some final rules of the road before sending you off to new adventures.

SOME FUTURE DESTINATIONS

This section lists a few career planning tools you'll want to know about.

You've got a lot of ground to cover in this phase of your career planning journey. Start your engines and get ready for an exciting adventure!

GET IN GEAR!

Career planning is a lifelong journey. There's usually more than one way to get where you're going, and there are often some interesting detours along the way. But, you have to start somewhere. So, rev up and find out all you can about you—one-of-a-kind, specially designed you. That's the first stop on what can be the most exciting trip of your life!

To get started, complete the two exercises described below.

WATCH FOR SIGNS ALONG THE WAY

Road signs help drivers figure out how to get where they want to go. They provide clues about direction, road conditions, and safety. Your career road signs will provide clues about who you are, what you like, and what you do best. These clues can help you decide where to look for the career ideas that are best for you.

Complete the following statements to make them true for you. There are no right or wrong answers. Jot down the response that describes you best. Your answers will provide important clues about career paths you should explore.

Please Note: If this book does not belong to you, write your responses on a separate sheet of paper.

On my last report card, I got the best grade in _____ .

On my last report card, I got the worst grade in _____ .

I am happiest when _____ .

Something I can do for hours without getting bored is _____ .

Something that bores me out of my mind is _____ .

My favorite class is _____ .

My least favorite class is _____ .

The one thing I'd like to accomplish with my life is _____ .

My favorite thing to do after school is __ .

My least favorite thing to do after school is _____ .

Something I'm really good at is _____ .

Something that is really tough for me to do is _____ .

My favorite adult person is _____ because _____ .

When I grow up _____ .

The kinds of books I like to read are about _____ .

The kinds of videos I like to watch are about _____ .

GET SOME DIRECTION

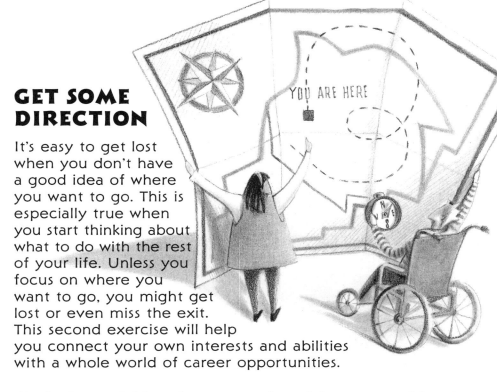

It's easy to get lost when you don't have a good idea of where you want to go. This is especially true when you start thinking about what to do with the rest of your life. Unless you focus on where you want to go, you might get lost or even miss the exit. This second exercise will help you connect your own interests and abilities with a whole world of career opportunities.

Mark the activities that you enjoy doing or would enjoy doing if you had the chance. Be picky. Don't mark ideas that you wish you would do, mark only those that you would really do. For instance, if the idea of skydiving sounds appealing, but you'd never do it because you are terrified of heights, don't mark it.

Please Note: If this book does not belong to you, write your responses on a separate sheet of paper.

- ❏ 1. Rescue a cat stuck in a tree
- ❏ 2. Visit the pet store every time you go to the mall
- ❏ 3. Paint a mural on the cafeteria wall
- ❏ 4. Run for student council
- ❏ 5. Send e-mail to a "pen pal" in another state
- ❏ 6. Survey your classmates to find out what they do after school
- ❏ 7. Try out for the school play
- ❏ 8. Dissect a frog and identify the different organs
- ❏ 9. Play baseball, soccer, football, or _____ (fill in your favorite sport)

❏ 10. Talk on the phone to just about anyone who will talk back

❏ 11. Try foods from all over the world—Thailand, Poland, Japan, etc.

❏ 12. Write poems about things that are happening in your life

❏ 13. Create a really scary haunted house to take your friends through on Halloween

❏ 14. Recycle all your family's trash

❏ 15. Bake a cake and decorate it for your best friend's birthday

❏ 16. Sell enough advertisements for the school yearbook to win a trip to Walt Disney World

❏ 17. Simulate an imaginary flight through space on your computer screen

❏ 18. Build model airplanes, boats, doll houses, or anything from kits

❏ 19. Teach your friends a new dance routine

❏ 20. Watch the stars come out at night and see how many constellations you can find

❏ 21. Watch baseball, soccer, football, or _____ (fill in your favorite sport) on TV

❏ 22. Give a speech in front of the entire school

❏ 23. Plan the class field trip to Washington, D.C.

❏ 24. Read everything in sight, including the back of the cereal box

❏ 25. Figure out "who dunnit" in a mystery story

❏ 26. Take in stray or hurt animals

❏ 27. Make a poster announcing the school football game

❏ 28. Think up a new way to make the lunch line move faster and explain it to the cafeteria staff

❏ 29. Put together a multimedia show for a school assembly using music and lots of pictures and graphics

❏ 30. Invest your allowance in the stock market and keep track of how it does

❏ 31. Go to the ballet or opera every time you get the chance

❏ 32. Do experiments with a chemistry set

❏ 33. Keep score at your sister's Little League game

- ❏ 34. Use lots of funny voices when reading stories to children
- ❏ 35. Ride on airplanes, trains, boats—anything that moves
- ❏ 36. Interview the new exchange student for an article in the school newspaper
- ❏ 37. Build your own treehouse
- ❏ 38. Help clean up a waste site in your neighborhood
- ❏ 39. Visit an art museum and pick out your favorite painting
- ❏ 40. Play Monopoly® in an all-night championship challenge
- ❏ 41. Make a chart on the computer to show how much soda students buy from the school vending machines each week
- ❏ 42. Keep track of how much your team earns to buy new uniforms
- ❏ 43. Play an instrument in the school band or orchestra
- ❏ 44. Put together a 1,000-piece puzzle
- ❏ 45. Write stories about sports for the school newspaper
- ❏ 46. Listen to other people talk about their problems
- ❏ 47. Imagine yourself in exotic places
- ❏ 48. Hang around bookstores and libraries
- ❏ 49. Play harmless practical jokes on April Fools' Day

❏ 50. Join the 4-H club at your school
❏ 51. Take photographs at the school talent show
❏ 52. Make money by setting up your own business—paper route, lemonade stand, etc.
❏ 53. Create an imaginary city using a computer
❏ 54. Do 3-D puzzles
❏ 55. Keep track of the top 10 songs of the week
❏ 56. Train your dog to do tricks
❏ 57. Make play-by-play announcements at the school football game
❏ 58. Answer the phones during a telethon to raise money for orphans
❏ 59. Be an exchange student in another country
❏ 60. Write down all your secret thoughts and favorite sayings in a journal
❏ 61. Jump out of an airplane (with a parachute, of course)
❏ 62. Plant and grow a garden in your backyard (or on your windowsill)
❏ 63. Use a video camera to make your own movies
❏ 64. Get your friends together to help clean up your town after a hurricane
❏ 65. Spend your summer at a computer camp learning lots of new computer programs

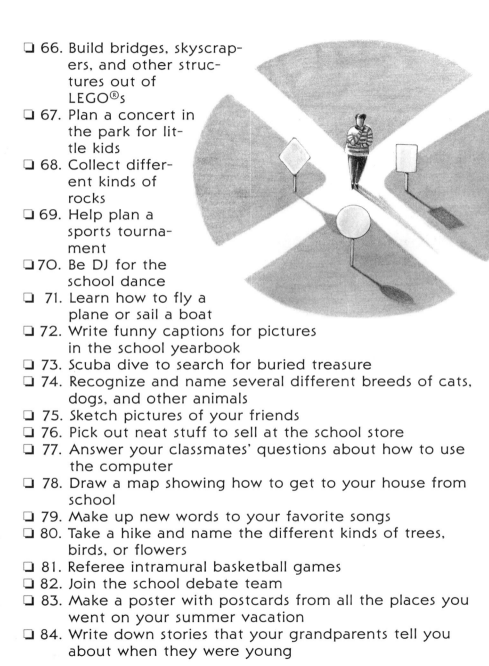

- ❏ 66. Build bridges, skyscrapers, and other structures out of LEGO®s
- ❏ 67. Plan a concert in the park for little kids
- ❏ 68. Collect different kinds of rocks
- ❏ 69. Help plan a sports tournament
- ❏ 70. Be DJ for the school dance
- ❏ 71. Learn how to fly a plane or sail a boat
- ❏ 72. Write funny captions for pictures in the school yearbook
- ❏ 73. Scuba dive to search for buried treasure
- ❏ 74. Recognize and name several different breeds of cats, dogs, and other animals
- ❏ 75. Sketch pictures of your friends
- ❏ 76. Pick out neat stuff to sell at the school store
- ❏ 77. Answer your classmates' questions about how to use the computer
- ❏ 78. Draw a map showing how to get to your house from school
- ❏ 79. Make up new words to your favorite songs
- ❏ 80. Take a hike and name the different kinds of trees, birds, or flowers
- ❏ 81. Referee intramural basketball games
- ❏ 82. Join the school debate team
- ❏ 83. Make a poster with postcards from all the places you went on your summer vacation
- ❏ 84. Write down stories that your grandparents tell you about when they were young

CALCULATE THE CLUES

Now is your chance to add it all up. Each of the 12 boxes on these pages contains an interest area that is common to both your world and the world of work. Follow these directions to discover your personal Skill Set:

1. Find all of the numbers that you checked on pages 9–13 in the boxes below and X them. Work your way all the way through number 84.
2. Go back and count the Xs marked for each interest area. Write that number in the space that says "total."
3. Find the interest area with the highest total and put a number one in the "Rank" blank of that box. Repeat this process for the next two highest scoring areas. Rank the second highest as number two and the third highest as number three.
4. If you have more than three strong areas, choose the three that are most important and interesting to you.

Remember: If this book does not belong to you, write your responses on a separate sheet of paper.

ADVENTURE	ANIMALS & NATURE	ART
❑ 1	❑ 2	❑ 3
❑ 13	❑ 14	❑ 15
❑ 25	❑ 26	❑ 27
❑ 37	❑ 38	❑ 39
❑ 49	❑ 50	❑ 51
❑ 61	❑ 62	❑ 63
❑ 73	❑ 74	❑ 75
Total: _____	Total: _____	Total: _____
Rank: _____	Rank: _____	Rank: _____

BUSINESS

- ❏ 4
- ❏ 16
- ❏ 28
- ❏ 40
- ❏ 52
- ❏ 64
- ❏ 76
- Total: _____
- Rank: _____

COMPUTERS

- ❏ 5
- ❏ 17
- ❏ 29
- ❏ 41
- ❏ 53
- ❏ 65
- ❏ 77
- Total: _____
- Rank: _____

MATH

- ❏ 6
- ❏ 18
- ❏ 30
- ❏ 42
- ❏ 54
- ❏ 66
- ❏ 78
- Total: _____
- Rank: _____

MUSIC/DANCE

- ❏ 7
- ❏ 19
- ❏ 31
- ❏ 43
- ❏ 55
- ❏ 67
- ❏ 79
- Total: _____
- Rank: _____

SCIENCE

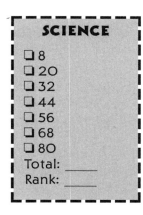

- ❏ 8
- ❏ 20
- ❏ 32
- ❏ 44
- ❏ 56
- ❏ 68
- ❏ 80
- Total: _____
- Rank: _____

SPORTS

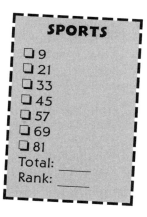

- ❏ 9
- ❏ 21
- ❏ 33
- ❏ 45
- ❏ 57
- ❏ 69
- ❏ 81
- Total: _____
- Rank: _____

TALKING

- ❏ 10
- ❏ 22
- ❏ 34
- ❏ 46
- ❏ 58
- ❏ 70
- ❏ 82
- Total: _____
- Rank: _____

TRAVEL

- ❏ 11
- ❏ 23
- ❏ 35
- ❏ 47
- ❏ 59
- ❏ 71
- ❏ 83
- Total: _____
- Rank: _____

WRITING

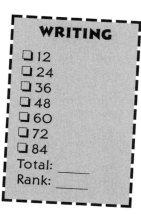

- ❏ 12
- ❏ 24
- ❏ 36
- ❏ 48
- ❏ 60
- ❏ 72
- ❏ 84
- Total: _____
- Rank: _____

What are your top three interest areas? List them here (or on a separate piece of paper).

1. _____

2. _____

3. _____

WRITE YOUR RESPONSES ON A SEPARATE PIECE OF PAPER

This is your personal Skill Set and provides important clues about the kinds of work you're most likely to enjoy. Remember it and look for career ideas with a skill set that matches yours most closely.

TAKE A TRIP!

Cruise down the career idea highway and enjoy in-depth profiles of some of the interesting options in this field. Keep in mind all that you've discovered about yourself so far. Find the careers that match your own Skill Set first. After that, keep on trucking through the other ideas—exploration is the name of this game.

There are countless ways to grow a career based on an interest in animals and nature. One of the best things about your interest is that many of the tools that you'd use on the job are all around you. Animals and plants are everywhere, just waiting for you to discover their wonders.

While many careers involving animals and nature require a strong science background, others require little more than a willingness to learn and work hard. You'll find lots of room for inventing creative career solutions.

As you read about the following careers, imagine yourself doing each job and ask yourself the following questions:

- 💡 Would I like it?
- 💡 Would I be good at it?
- 💡 Is it the stuff my career dreams are made of?

If so, make a quick exit to explore what it involves, try it out, check it out, and get acquainted!

Buckle up and enjoy the trip!

A NOTE ON WEBSITES

Internet sites tend to move around the Web a bit. If you have trouble finding a particular site, use an Internet browser to find a specific website or type of information.

Agribusiness Consultant

SKILL SET

✔ ANIMALS & NATURE

✔ BUSINESS

✔ TRAVEL

GO visit a food manufacturing plant to see how food is prepared for consumers like you.

READ all you can about your favorite foods and where they come from.

TRY making a list of all the jobs involved in getting food on your table. Start at the farm and take it from there. It should be a very long list!

WHAT IS AN AGRIBUSINESS CONSULTANT?

Two little words—*food* and *fiber*—describe an industry that employs millions of people worldwide. Agribusiness involves every food you eat and every thread of fabric you use for clothing and other items. Agribusiness includes any profession that combines agricultural interests with expertise in management, finance, accounting, marketing, manufacturing, or other types of business functions.

Agribusiness goes far beyond farming; it involves the production, processing, and distribution of food, feed, and fiber. It also includes the network of services that support production, processing, and distribution, such as transportation, storage, credit and finance, insurance, manufacturing, research and development, and government regulation and inspection.

Agribusiness is big, and it offers a world of opportunity for men and women alike. It's so big that food and fiber production, manufacturing and the associated marketing, finance, retailing, and service industries make agriculture the largest employer in the United States. The industry is so big, in fact, that the U.S. Department of Agriculture estimates that there are many more agribusiness careers than there are qualified people to fill them. All this provides ample opportunities for experts in the field.

The field is also as diverse as it is big. Common entry-level positions include grain merchandiser, agricultural chemical representative, commodity broker, agricultural loan officer, farm supply manager, flour mill manager, meat marketing manager, feedlot manager, and livestock pharmaceutical product representative. And that's just the beginning. With the right training and experience, you can pursue professions that involve all manner of business expertise, from law or economics to marketing or sales.

Another exciting consideration is the possibility of experiencing worldwide, or at least nationwide, travel in your career. Food and fiber are international concerns, so there are opportunities in literally every corner of the world.

Careers in agribusiness require specialized training. Although opportunities abound at any level of the education spectrum, from high school diploma to Ph.D., most of the jobs require a four-year college degree. Many colleges now offer agricultural business majors that combine coursework in agricultural economics, business, and agricultural technology.

Agribusiness is an industry in which you can custom tailor a career based on your own interests and strengths. It's one that offers almost limitless opportunities for professional growth in a fascinating field. It's a career path that combines highly practical business sense with the noble cause of feeding the world. Not bad for a day's work!

TRY IT OUT

FUN ON THE FARM

Help yourself to some fun facts and entertaining activities while you learn more about agriculture at some of these websites.

- North Carolina Department of Agriculture and Consumer Services' Kids World at http://www.agr.state.nc.us/cyber/kidswrld
- United States Department of Agriculture's Fun Stuff at http://www.usda.gov/nass/nasskids/games/games2.htm
- National Agricultural Statistics Service's NASS Kids http://www.usda.gov/nass/nasskids/nasskids.htm

DOWN AND DIRTY

Once you've had enough of the kid stuff, take a look at some of the resources that agribusiness consultants use to do their jobs. As is true of so many professions, good information is key to success. Here are some sources of the best agribusiness information you'll find anywhere.

☀ *The Agriculture Fact Book,* an annual publication of the U.S. Department of Agriculture, is accessible on-line at http://www.usda.gov/news/pubs/fbook98/content.htm.

☀ *The State of the Land* is the Department of Agriculture's index to agricultural maps, facts, and figures. It is available at http://www.nhq.nrcs.usda.gov/land/index/intro. html.

☀ *The State of Food and Agriculture (SOFA)* is an annual report on world agriculture put out by the United Nations' Food and Agriculture Organization. It can be accessed at http://www.fao.org/waicent/faoinfo/ economic/esa/sofa.htm.

While you're on the Internet, pick a particular crop, such as pineapple, and a part of the world, such as the Philippines, and see if you can find out using a search engine why the place and the product are made for each other. Start with one website and keep snooping until you find some answers.

MEET YOUR FUTURE EMPLOYER

To get an idea of the many different kinds of job opportunities available in agribusiness, check out the Agribusiness Career Page (http://www.cba.unl.edu/student/agmba/page4. html). This site provides links to many of the big U.S. agribusiness employers such as Campbell Soup Company, John Deere farm equipment company, and Frito-Lay snack company. Visit several companies and try to imagine yourself working at each one. What kinds of jobs sound most appealing to you?

AGRIBUSINESS 101

Thanks to the folks at Mississippi State University, you can treat yourself to a world-class education in agribusiness from the comfort of your home or school computer desk. They have developed a series of lessons designed to acquaint middle school and high school students with agribusiness in a global environment. Take a peek at http://www.ais.msstate. edu/AGE/about.html.

GROW SOME KNOWLEDGE
Some resources for finding additional information about agribusiness careers include

Smith, Marcella, Jean M. Underwood, and Archie Augustus
Stone. *Careers in Agribusiness.* Danville, Ill.: Interstate
Publishers, 1991.
White, William C., Donald N. Collins, and Adrian A. Paradis.
Opportunities in Farming and Agriculture Careers.
Lincolnwood, Ill.: VGM Career Horizons, 1995.

SHOP TILL YOU DROP
Agribusiness encompasses a wide variety of products. Some you can eat; some you can't. To get an idea of the diverse nature of this industry, take off on an Internet shopping excursion. Give yourself a budget of a cool one million bucks and see what you can buy to set up a farm or ranch of your own. Warm up your shopping cart at http://www. agrimall.com.

GOOD STUFF FOR SALE
One of the challenges facing any type of agribusiness is getting people to buy the products being sold. That makes marketing and sales an important part of the industry. Two campaigns in particular have done a masterful job of getting their products out to the masses: milk and beef. Visit these websites and see what you can learn from their success: http://www.whymilk.com, http://www.got-milk.com, and http://www.beef.org.

Now pick an agricultural product that is widely used by people your age (several junk food items may come to mind). Come up with a catchy ad campaign that would make more kids want to buy your product. Make a poster and other types of advertising materials to get your point across.

CHECK IT OUT

American Agricultural Economics Association
415 South Duff Avenue, Suite C
Ames, Iowa 50010-6600
http://www.aaea.org

American Farm Bureau
224 West Touhy Avenue
Park Ridge, Illinois 60068
http://www.fb.com

American Society of Agricultural Consultants
950 South Cherry Street, Suite 508
Denver, Colorado 80246-2664
http://www.agri-associations.org/asac

Council for Agricultural Science and Technology
4420 West Lincoln Way
Ames, Iowa 50014-3447
http://www.cast-science.org

Food Marketing Institute
800 Connecticut Avenue NW, Suite 400
Washington, D.C. 20006
http://www.fmi.org

International Food and Agribusiness Management Association
Department of Agricultural Economics
Texas A&M University
College Station, Texas 77843-2124
http://www.ifama.org

International Food Information Council Foundation
1100 Connecticut Avenue NW, Suite 430
Washington, D.C. 20036
http://ificinfo.health.org

United States Department of Agriculture
1400 Independence Avenue SW
Washington, D.C. 20250-0233
http://www.usda.gov

GET ACQUAINTED

Dean Wheeler,
Agribusiness Consultant

CAREER PATH

CHILDHOOD ASPIRATION: To be an agricultural extension agent.

FIRST JOB: Living in a hog barn taking care of pigs during college.

CURRENT JOB: Founder of AgResults, Inc., an agribusiness consulting firm.

BORN TO THE JOB

Dean Wheeler grew up on a farm and learned to love all things agricultural. The idea to become a county extension agent (someone who works with farmers and 4-H programs) struck him at an early age. Two things helped encourage this interest. First, his mother worked for the county extension service and had nothing but good things to say about it. He saw firsthand how the advice given by their county extension agents helped their family's farm thrive.

The second reason was 4-H clubs. Wheeler joined his local club as soon as he was eligible to participate at the age of 10 and stayed active until he reached the maximum age limit of 21. The experience shaped his life in many ways. He learned the responsibilities of caring for animals through projects that involved raising lambs, calves, and other young animals. He learned how to relate to other people by helping younger club members with their projects. He learned how to manage money by raising a steer for the county fair. (His steer was chosen grand champion of the fair, and Wheeler made money for college that year.) Also Wheeler learned valuable leadership skills by serving in various roles as a club officer. It was time well spent.

ALOHA, PINEAPPLES!

During his years at college, Wheeler's plan was still to become an extension agent; however, during his senior year, Del Monte, one of the food industry giants, offered him a job working with pineapples in Hawaii. Newly married and game for an adventure, both Wheeler and his wife thought spending a few years in Hawaii would be a fun way to start their life together.

Wheeler began his career in the research department learning nearly all there was to know about pineapples. He moved on to manage a 2,000-acre section of the company's pineapple plantation on the island of Oahu. A couple of years later, he was assigned to manage the equipment on a plantation that was located on the island of Molokai and produced 100,000 tons of pineapples a year. Living on this remote island offered Wheeler and his family a chance to enjoy Hawaii at its best—with plenty of beaches, waterfalls, and luaus (Hawaiian feasts) to keep them busy.

OFF TO SEE THE WORLD

Wheeler's next career move was a big one. When Del Monte decided to start a new pineapple plantation in Kenya, Wheeler decided he was the man for the job.

Wheeler arrived in Kenya, hired 10 Kenyans, and began digging the fields for the new plantation. The only problem was that he spoke English and his workers spoke Kiswahili. Luckily, Wheeler was a quick learner and Kiswahili is a relatively easy language to learn. With lots of homework and plenty of embarrassing mistakes, Wheeler was chatting away in Kiswahili within six months. By the time he left Kenya, the plantation had grown to include 10,000 acres, a cannery had been built, and the pineapple business was booming.

The next stop in Wheeler's global career was the Philippines, followed by a stint in Costa Rica. After 26 years of living overseas, Wheeler decided to come home to his native country, the United States. He was assigned to Miami but didn't spend much time there. Instead, he traveled the world to places such as Peru, Puerto Rico, Jamaica, and Brazil in search of new sources of pineapples, mangoes, papaya, and other exotic fruits.

A WAY WITH CROPS

After working with Del Monte for 33 years, Wheeler put his vast resources and rich experience to work in his own agribusiness consulting firm: AgResults, Inc. Technically, Wheeler still lives in Miami, but he's always on the go. During the first few years of business, Wheeler has already made 25 trips to Mexico, 10 to Ecuador, 5 to Puerto Rico, and 6 to Equatorial Guinea, as well as trips to Guatemala, Colombia, Peru, Brazil, Venezuela, Spain, and the Ivory Coast. One of his proudest moments so far was going back to the still flourishing company he had helped to start in Kenya to advise them on some new agricultural opportunities.

THE INSIDE TRACK

According to Wheeler, an effective agribusiness consultant needs a good education and practical experience. He says that young people considering such a career should plan on starting with a corporation, consulting firm, or other group that has experienced people from whom a newcomer can learn. After a few years of working with someone else, a person has the professional and interpersonal skills that make for a successful consultant.

FREE ADVICE

As an agribusiness consultant, Wheeler travels the world helping a wide variety of agricultural enterprises to succeed. The product he "sells" is his good advice. He's got some free advice for you, though. He says the best thing you can do to prepare for a career like his is to get involved. It doesn't matter if it's a 4-H club, Future Farmers of America, the Boy Scouts, or whatever. Just get involved and watch your skills grow!

Animal Trainer

WHAT IS AN ANIMAL TRAINER?

Animal trainers have been around for thousands of years. Camels were trained to act as moving vans; dogs, to pull sleds; and birds, to hunt food for their owner's dinner table. Today, many different kinds of animals are taught to do special things. Pigs become movie stars, dogs help people see and hear or assist police, cats provide comfort to the elderly, and dolphins and whales help reveal the mysteries of the deep sea.

Patience and persistence are the most important requirements for an animal trainer. An animal trainer spends lots of time working with many different animals, whether they be dogs, cats, and other house pets or more exotic animals such as potbellied pigs, lions, elephants, fish, and chickens.

Animal trainers work in many different places. Some animal trainers work with pet owners teaching basic obedience skills. Other animal trainers specialize in horses and spend their days at ranches, stables, or equestrian centers. Still others work in aquariums to train dolphins and whales to respond to commands. Some even work on the sets of movies that feature or even star animal characters. Imagine teaching pigs to dance or working with an entire menagerie of talented animals!

In addition, there are other highly specialized types of animal training. For instance, some animal trainers train dogs to help people with disabilities, such as the visually or hearing impaired. Other dogs are trained to assist those confined to a wheelchair. These dogs learn to provide companionship and practical physical help and literally to be lifesavers.

Another specialty is training police dogs. This could involve training dogs to sniff out drugs or bombs or to lead manhunts for criminals or lost people. As you might imagine, it takes a smart animal and an exceptional trainer to succeed in these tasks.

If an animal has the physical and mental ability to do a task, however unusual, it can be trained to do it. Trainers use a technique called positive reinforcement to change an animal's behavior. Good parents use the same strategy. It involves rewarding good behavior with treats or praise. For instance, Fido gets a biscuit when he "sits" on command, while Johnny gets an allowance for doing his chores or Patty gets taken out to dinner for doing well on her test.

Education requirements for animal trainers vary widely depending on the situation. No degree is required to train house pets; however, the more you know about animals and how to make them behave, the more likely you are to succeed. Books, special training courses offered through parks and recreation departments, and some vocational programs may provide the initial training you need to get started. Experience is the best teacher in this type of work. Training your own pets and volunteering at animal shelters are good ways to build skills.

On the other hand, if you want to train dolphins at SeaWorld or animals at a zoo, a degree in animal behavior (sometimes called ethology), biology, or oceanography is necessary. Any experience you can get along the way is also helpful in this competitive field.

There is nothing quite as satisfying as sharing time with a well-behaved animal. Being an animal trainer can be a great way to make a living if you are a patient, consistent, adventurous animal lover.

TRY IT OUT

CLICK UP YOUR HEELS!

Some animal trainers recommend using a clicker to reinforce certain behaviors in dogs. A clicker is a simple device that makes a sound when you press it. You can make one out of any jar that has a freshness seal at the top. For information on how to make a clicker and how to use it to train a pet, go online to the ClickerTrain website at http://www.clickertrain.com.

MAKE A MAZE

If you have a hamster or a gerbil for a pet, you can try the old maze trick to test the positive reinforcement theory.

Using an old cardboard box, make a maze with several small corridors. Make sure that some routes lead to dead ends and others to an opening.

Place bits of your pet's favorite treat at the end of the maze. Put the animal at the beginning and see how long it takes to get to the end. Try placing bits of food at intervals along the correct route to see if you can shorten the time. See if practice makes perfect and the animal makes better time with subsequent tries.

TRAINING TOOLBOX

The Internet can be the source of both fun and facts while learning about training all kinds of animals. Here are a few sites to try.

- ☀ You can find stories and photos from animal trainers around the world at http://www.angelfire.com/az/clickryder/home.html.
- ☀ Look for the Doggie Repair Kit at http://www.clickandtreat.com.
- ☀ Find games, jokes, articles, and quizzes for horse lovers at http://www.adairmag.com.
- ☀ For more on horse training and some great reading look at http://www.horsemansarts.com.
- ☀ Have you ever wanted to train an iguana? Look at http://www.geocities.com/Heartland/Meadows/4159/training.html.
- ☀ Information about dolphin and whale training at SeaWorld can be found at http://www.seaworld.org/animal_training/mmtrain.html.
- ☀ To find out if your dog would make a good therapy dog, visit http://www.dog-play.com/therapy.html.
- ☀ Are you ready for some wacky fun? Try http://www.hamsterdance.com. It's guaranteed to drive everyone within hearing distance absolutely nuts!

READ ALL ABOUT IT!

There are tons of books on animal training and animal behavior. Here are a few to start with.

Donaldson, Jean. *The Culture Clash.* Berkeley, Calif.: James & Kenneth Publishers, 1996.

Kelley, Lydia. *Teamwork II: Dog Training Manual for People with Disabilities.* Tucson, Ariz.: Top Dog, 1998.

Pryor, Karen. *Clicker Magic.* New York: Bantam Books, 1999.

———. *A Dog and a Dolphin: An Introduction to Click & Treat Training.* North Bend, Wash.: Sunshine Books, 1999.

———. *Don't Shoot the Dog!* New York: Bantam Books, 1984.

CHECK IT OUT

American Kennel Club
260 Madison Avenue, Fourth Floor
New York, New York 10016
http://www.akc.org

Association of Pet Dog Trainers
P.O. Box 385
Davis, California 95617
http://www.apdt.com

International Marine Animal Trainers Association
1200 South Lake Shore Drive
Chicago, Illinois 60605

Performing Animal Welfare Society
P.O. Box 849
Galt, California 95632
http://www.pawsweb.org

The United States Combined Training Association
525 Old Waterford Road NW
Leesburg, Virginia 20176
http://www.hhhorse.com/USCTA/main.html

GET ACQUAINTED

Laura Bourhenne,
Animal Trainer

CAREER PATH

CHILDHOOD ASPIRATION: To train dolphins.

FIRST JOB: Working at a dough-nut shop.

CURRENT JOB: President of Animal Attraction Unlimited, a company that specializes in train-ing cats and dogs.

CONTROL FREAK

Laura Bourhenne is a self-confessed control freak. That's why she enjoys her work as an animal trainer so much. She says it is great to watch the "wheels turning" in animals' minds as they learn. Even more fun is getting them to think the way she wants them to think. That's where the control factor comes in. Training animals is all about getting them to do what *you* want them to do when *you* want them to do it.

This takes patience and lots of it. Taking things slowly and sys-tematically makes the training process easier. Understanding the wants and needs of the animal you are training also makes it easier. Animals love praise and treats. They need to be told how wonderful they are and they like eating tasty treats—but then, don't we all?

SMARTER THAN YOUR AVERAGE PIG (OR MONKEY)

In addition to caring for her own animals, Bourhenne loves to train potbellied pigs. These pigs are cleaner and neater than most dogs, and they learn faster. They have lots of personality. They're also more fun because they try to get away with things that dogs don't even think about trying. The pigs' main goal is to try to get the treat or reward without doing what Bourhenne wants them to do. Being smarter than a pig is sometimes a challenge! Bourhenne says the downside of pigs for pets is they can be destructive, and—as only a pig can do—they can get awfully big.

The most difficult animal Bourhenne has ever worked with was a male vervet monkey she had to train. It was frustrating because, while he liked men and would do almost anything for the male trainers, he didn't like women. He did everything he could to hurt her feelings and make training impossible—but she finally won out in the end.

TRAINING ON WHEELS

Bourhenne spends most of her day at her customers' homes training their dogs and preparing them for obedience school. She works a lot with dogs that tend to be aggressive. Training the animals is easy. The hard part is training their owner!

A typical visit involves simple, preparatory tasks such as housebreaking the dog and teaching the dog to walk on a leash and to obey commands such as "sit," "heel," and the ever popular "no."

Once animals master a few basic commands, they are ready for a full obedience class with another trainer. Here they interact with other dogs and owners and learn how to do more advanced tricks.

JUST DO IT!

Bourhenne didn't always know she wanted to be an animal trainer; in fact, it wasn't until after three years of college studying physical therapy that she decided animal training was for her. So she looked for a training program that would give her the credibility she needed to succeed. There was a lot of competition to get into the school she wanted to attend, and she almost talked herself out of applying! But she hung in there, got in, and the rest is history.

Bourhenne suggests that future animal trainers get started now. There are lots of things you can do to get comfortable with animals. She suggests volunteering for a rescue organization to get experience handling animals. She offers one warning, however. Don't fall in love with the animals. It is enough to know that you are making a difference and learning about animal behavior at the same time. You can't take them all home!

Arborist

WHAT IS AN ARBORIST?

Tree doctor is the best way to describe an arborist's work. According to the National Arborist Association, an arborist is "a professional who cares for trees and other woody plants by pruning, fertilizing, monitoring for insects and diseases, consulting on tree related issues, and occasionally planting, transplanting, and removing trees."

Arborists are keepers of the trees. They work their own brand of magic mostly in people's yards and at places of business, but they may also work in forests, public gardens, parks, historic sites, and national forests. To understand the imporant role that trees play in our world, think back to one of your very first science lessons about photosynthesis. Arborists not only make trees look pretty, they also help perserve valuable sources of life-sustaining oxygen. By protecting trees, arborists also protect the environment, because trees are a natural filter of air pollutants. The yummy fruits and nuts that grow on trees are an added bonus! When you look at the big picture like this, it's easy to see why the world needs arborists, and plenty of them.

Success in this profession requires enjoying and appreciating trees. Trees are the number-one customer of this business, so an arborist has to be well acquainted with many different kinds of trees. Since trees are often attached in one way or another to people, however, it's also important that arborists enjoy working with people. In addition, arborists need to be physically fit and must be prepared to work outdoors in all types of weather.

Arborists are employed in a variety of settings. Two of the biggest employers are businesses that serve residential and commercial customers, and public utility companies. Asplundh Tree Expert Company, the largest tree care firm in the world, employs more than 21,000 arborists to service various utility companies around the world. City governments, recreation centers, and state and national parks are also possible employers.

Botanical gardens and arboretums (which are "museums" and "laboratories" for plant life) also employ arborists to collect, maintain, and preserve trees from all over the world.

Arboriculture is a field with plenty of opportunity for nature fanatics with an entrepreneurial bent. Many arborists combine a love of trees with running their own businesses in ventures that include tree farms, nurseries, and commercial or residential yard care. Some companies are small with just one or two employees serving a small geographic area, while others may grow to employ thousands of people and have branch offices in far-flung places, such as Australia and Europe, as well as any number of states within the United States.

Judging from the results of a 1997 Gallup poll, tree and lawn care is big business in America. The survey found that more than 22 million U.S. households have spent more than $14 million on professional landscape, lawn care, and tree services every year since 1993. With statistics such as those that follow, it's plain to see that arborists keep busy performing services that include

- caring for 23 million trees in the United States
- pruning 13 million trees
- fertilizing 3 million trees
- treating 6 million trees for insects
- treating 2 million trees for disease

There are several ways to get started as an arborist. You might opt to enroll in a two- or four-year arboriculture or horticulture program at a college or university. If you want to dig right in and get started in this career, you might seek out a commercial tree company that would be willing to provide on-the-job training as an apprentice. Another option is to enroll in a home study program offered by official organizations such as the National Arborist Association.

Whichever educational route you choose, you may also want to consider becoming a certified arborist. This credential, administered by the International Society of Arboriculture, helps lend credibility to your skills and professional commitment. To become certified you must have at least three years experience in arboriculture and must pass a test that covers information such as tree biology, tree nutrition and fertilization, and diagnosis and treatment of tree problems.

If you're looking for a growing profession, a career in trees might be worth a serious look.

TRY IT OUT

BIRD'S-EYE VIEW
Tree Care Industry is a monthly publication of the National Arborist Association and is what in-the-know arborists read to stay current with their profession. For a free issue, contact the National Arborist Association by mail at P.O. Box 1094, Amherst, New Hampshire 03031-1094, or via the Internet at http://www.natlarb.com/tci.htm.

TAKE A VIRTUAL HIKE!
Trees come in all kinds of shapes, sizes, and varieties. If trees are in your future, you might as well start getting acquainted with some of the fascinating species that await your tender care. While there's no substitute for actually getting outside and investigating the real thing, you can find some great background information on the Internet at sites such as the following:

- Arboriculture On-line at http://www2.champaign. isa-arbor.com
- Amazing Trees at http://www.suite101.com/welcome. cfm/trees
- TreeWeb at http://www.quercus.uky.edu/treeweb/ index.htm
- PLANTS National Database at http://plants.usda.gov/
- National Arbor Day Foundation at http://www.arborday. org
- Tree Silhouettes at http://www.domtar.com/arbre/ english/index.htm

When you're ready to connect what you've learned on-line with what you can find outdoors, be sure to take along a nature field guide. Find one that you like at your local library or try this highly recommended one: *National Audubon Society Field Guide to North American Trees* by Elbert Little (New York: Alfred A. Knopf, 1996).

TREE TALK

Trees have a language all their own, and some of the words get pretty complicated. For instance, do you have any idea what any of the following words mean?

adventitious	deciduous	photosynthesis
arboreal	heliophilious	sucker
cambium		

To learn the lingo, use a dictionary, go on-line to http://www.domtar.com/arbre/english/glossair.htm, or consult David Evans' *Terms of the Trade: A Reference for the Forest Products* (Eugene, Oreg.: Random Lengths Publications, 1993). Consider keeping track of your new vocabulary in a small notebook or on index cards.

Tree Sleuths

If you are interested in learning more about trees and other woody plants, join the club—the American Association of Amateur Arborists "club." Check out their Internet website for ideas on hosting an arbor walk, to request free arbor tags to label trees in your community, and to learn how to make an arbor map. To find out more, visit the association's website at http://www.arborworks.org.

Treetop Fun

Learning about trees can be fun through games available at these websites.

☀ National Wildlife Federation Games at http://www.nwf. org/nwf/games

❧ Forest Are for Kids at http://www.idahoforests.org/kids1.htm
❧ Go exploring in the Fantastic Forest at http://www.nationalgeographic.com/forest/
❧ World of Trees at http://www.domtar.com/arbre/english/start.htm

CHECK IT OUT

American Forests
P.O. Box 2000
Washington, D.C. 20013
http://www.amfor.org

American Society of Consulting Arborists
5130 West 101st Circle
Westminster, Colorado 80030

International Society of Arboriculture
P.O. Box GG
Savoy, Illinois 61874
http://www2.champaign.isa-arbor.com

National Arbor Day Foundation
100 Arbor Avenue
Nebraska City, Nebraska 68410
http://www.arborday.org

National Arborist Association
P.O. Box 1094
Amherst, New Hampshire 03031-1094
http://www.natlarb.com

Society of American Foresters
5400 Grosvenor Lane
Bethesda, Maryland 20814
http://www.safnet.org

Society of Commercial Arboriculture
P.O. Box 3129
Champaign, Illinois 61826
http://www.aces.uiuc.edu/~isa-sca

GET ACQUAINTED

Don Blair,
Arborist

CAREER PATH

CHILDHOOD ASPIRATION: To work in a pickle factory near his boyhood home.

FIRST JOB: Working a paper route, painting houses, and doing other odd jobs.

CURRENT JOB: Consulting arborist and CEO of Sierra Moreno Mercantile Company.

THE FAMILY TREE

Trees have always been a way of life for Don Blair. His father, Millard Blair, founded a tree care company back in 1922 and owned it until his death in 1984. Even before he was old enough to spell *tree,* the younger Blair was earning income from trees. That's because his father designated funds from specific parts of the family tree business to each of his children. One daughter earned money from the fruit of their cherry trees; another earned money from the nuts of their walnut trees. For Blair it was firewood. He says he got the best deal of the three because when the cherry and walnut trees died, he removed them and made money off of firewood from his sisters' trees too. By the time he was in high school, he had earned enough to pay cash for a brand-new pickup truck.

During high school, Blair had big plans for life after graduation, and they didn't involve trees. After a successful stint as backstage producer for the Miss California pageant in 1971, Blair was invited to reprise his role for the Miss America pageant in Atlantic City. He was certain that this was just the first stop on his way to a bright future in theater. He literally had his bags packed and was ready to go.

Fate had other plans for him, however. Just days before he was scheduled to leave, his father became very ill. Blair was faced with an important decision. Leave and make it on his own, or stay and keep the family business running. He stayed, his dad got better, and Blair began an exciting career that has grown in ways he never dared imagine back then.

PROMISES TO KEEP

Blair may have given up his theatrical dreams for trees, but he didn't do it without some strings attached. He knew there was more to trees than just dragging brush through a chipper, so he promised himself to make it as interesting as possible. He vowed to take advantage of every opportunity and to create new ones every chance he got. Blair has been as good as his word for more than 25 years now.

He started working for his dad's company in 1971. His first job was as a climber, and due to some quick learning and hard work, he was soon promoted to crew foreman. It took only a few years to assume the role of general manager of the entire business. Of course, things can get a bit weird when your father is also your boss. Blair remembers with a smile that he was either fired or quit at least three or four times in his career, but he was always rehired before he had to find another job.

THE RIGHT PLACE AT THE RIGHT TIME

Always mindful of keeping his earlier promise to himself, Blair took advantage of a particularly "slow" winter one year to launch a new company. The Sierra Moreno Mercantile Company was created to distribute and sell supplies, tools, and safety equipment for arborists.

Until then the only means that West Coast arborists had of getting work supplies was to order them from East Coast companies. Blair's new business gave them easier and quicker access to the tools they needed to get their jobs done. As the only business in town that catered especially to arborists, Blair's business thrived.

HAVE TREE KNOW-HOW, WILL TRAVEL

When Blair's father died in 1984, Blair took over as owner of the tree service company. He ran it until 1988 when he decided it was time to pursue new opportunities in the tree industry. He sold the original business and founded the M. F. Blair Institute of Arboriculture (named after his father). Through the institute, Blair provides consulting and training services and indulges in his passion for preserving the history of arboriculture.

Through this venture, Blair started sharing his expertise in areas such as aerial rescue; rope and saddle climbing techniques; hazard tree evaluation; large-scale tree pruning; cabling, bracing, and guying; and felling techniques. This work has taken him all over the United States as well as to other countries around the world. He says that 25 years ago he never would've imagined that people would pay him to talk about tree removal in places such as Australia, England, and Germany.

For an inside look at some of Blair's areas of expertise, check out his book *Arborist Equipment: A Guide to the Tools and Equipment of Tree Maintenance and Removal* (Savoy, Ill.: International Society of Arborists, 1995).

GUARANTEED SUCCESS

Through all his endeavors, Blair has learned a few secrets of success that he believes will work for any businessperson. He says you can count on succeeding if you do these three things:

Answer your phone.

Keep your appointments.

Do what you said you'd do at the price you said you'd do it for.

Blair says to never stop learning and growing with your profession. Learning not only keeps you on top of changes in your chosen field, but it keeps the work fresh and interesting as well.

It's worked for Blair. Give it a try and see if it works for you!

Botanist

SKILL SET

✔ ANIMALS & NATURE

✔ SCIENCE

✔ ADVENTURE

GO visit a botanical garden or arboretum.

READ some of the gardening magazines available at your local library or newsstand.

TRY planting some flowers in your backyard or in a windowsill.

WHAT IS A BOTANIST?

A botanist is a plant scientist. If it's green and growing, a botanist works with it. A botanist's work might involve unlocking the mysteries of a tiny bacterial cell or teaching farmers in developing nations how to grow herbs for medicine. The career options in botany are as varied as the plants a botanist works with.

One common botanical work scenario involves conducting research for scientific purposes or for solving ecological problems. Another involves work in public gardens to create beautiful nature museums. Still another scenario involves developing commercial products, such as medicines, foods, fibers, and building supplies.

Colleges and universities are the number-one employer of botanists. Teaching and research are the main tasks associated with botanists working in an academic setting. Federal and state government agencies such as the U.S. Department of Agriculture, the National Park Service, and even the National Aeronautics and Space Agency (NASA) come in as the number-two employer of botanists. Industries such as drug companies, the oil industry, lumber and paper companies, seed and nursery companies, fruit growers, and food companies are the third largest type of employer of botanists. In addition, with food and pollution issues always a worldwide concern, there are a number of ways to add an international flavor to a career in botany.

If all those botanical opportunities aren't enough, people with an interest in plants and flowers can consider these additional types of applied plant science:

agronomy, which applies the science of raising crops to the business of running a farm.

biotechnology, a hot area of innovation that uses biological organisms to produce useful new products.

forestry, which includes forest management, timber production, and conservation.

herbal research, a growing field that involves using herbs to develop medicines, foods, cosmetics, and other "natural" products.

horticulture, which involves working with plants to create beautiful and useful gardens.

plant pathology, which concerns diseases of plants.

With a field so diverse, education and training requirements vary widely. For instance, some positions at plant nurseries and botanical gardens require little more than a green thumb, a thorough understanding of plant care, and a willingness to "get down and dirty" while taking care of plants.

As in other professions with a strong science emphasis, however, the more you know, the more ways your career can grow. Count on earning at least a four-year bachelor's degree in college to prepare for research and commercial types of botany. Depending on the focus of your intended work, you may find that advanced degrees may eventually become necessary as well.

Budding botanists can get a jump start on their career ambitions by taking notice of the green and growing things all around them. Opportunities to learn are as close as your own backyard, a nearby park, or a well-stocked flower shop. Dig in and grow yourself a great career!

TRY IT OUT

GET A JOB!
Put your green thumb and your interest in plant life to the test during your summer vacations and after school. Parks, campgrounds, plant nurseries, health food stores, farms, florists, or landscaping and yard care companies are always in need of good, strong help. Find a job and get paid to learn about plants!

MESSING AROUND WITH PLANTS
There's nothing like the real thing when it comes to plants; however, you may find that a little high technology helps comes in handy when you are trying to learn your way around the different varieties of plants. Some Internet sites to explore for information, activities, and general fun and games include

- The Great Plant Escape at http://www.urbanext. uiuc.edu/gpe/
- Sci4Kids at http://www.ars.usda.gov/is/kids
- USDA-NASS Kids Games Page at http://www.usda.gov/ nass/nasskids/games/games2.htm

BUDDING BOTANISTS

You're never too young to get started as a botanist. All you need is an inquisitive mind, some scientific curiosity, a little help from a trusted adult, and a few good ideas for experiments. Green thumb is optional. Use books like these to get started.

Bleifeld, Maurice. *Botany Projects for Young Scientists.* Danbury, Conn.: Franklin Watts, 1992.

Dashefsky, H. Steven. *Botany: High School Science Fair Experiments.* New York: McGraw-Hill, 1994.

Hunken, Jorie. *Botany for All Ages: Discovering Nature Through Activities for Children and Adults.* Old Saybrook, Conn.: Globe Pequot Press, 1996.

Keen, Daniel, and Robert Bonnet. *Botany: 49 Science Fair Projects.* New York: McGraw-Hill, 1990.

If you can't find any of these resources, look for botany projects in general science experiment books.

BOTANIC HEROES

One way to get an idea of what your future in botany could be like is to read about others who have made their mark as botanists. Role models worth emulating are featured in books such as the following:

Adair, Gene. *George Washington Carver: Botanist.* Introduction by Coretta Scott King. New York: Chelsea House, 1990.

Davis, Wade. *One River: Explorations and Discoveries in the Amazon Rain Forest.* New York: Touchstone Books, 1997.

Tyler-Whittle, Michael Sidney. *The Plant Hunters: Great Botanist-Explorers and the Plants They Sought.* New York: Lyons & Burford, 1997.

See if you can find others and take note of the qualities that allowed these people to make lasting impressions as plant scientists.

HOW DOES YOUR GARDEN GROW?

Got dirt? Grow a garden! Just add seeds or seedlings, water, sunshine, and plenty of tender loving care to grow anything from cacti to cucumbers in your own backyard or windowsill.

Visit a plant nursery in your community to find out what types of plants grow best in your area or consult experts from around the world at some of these Internet sites.

- ☀ GardenWeb at http://www.gardenweb.com
- ☀ GardenNet at http://www.gardennet.com
- ☀ The Garden Gate at http://www.gardengatemag.com
- ☀ Garden.com at http://www.garden.com

GROW A VIRTUAL PLANT

For a more scientific exploration of plants, visit the Virtual Plants site at http://www.ctpm.uq.edu.au/virtualplants/ipivp.html. Here you'll find models of plants at various stages of development, and you can simulate the impact various types of factors such as pesticides or insects might have on a specific type of plant. The site gets a bit complicated but provides a good example of the research side of the profession.

LOOK IT UP!

Like any other scientific field, botany has its own lingo. You can start learning the language of plants at http://www.gardenweb.com/glossary. Here you'll find the definitions for more than 2,500 terms that include the following:

abiogenesis   adze

achlorphyllous   agamosporous

adenosine diphosphate

And that's just words beginning with *a!* Keep a log of all the interesting words you come across and watch your knowledge of botany grow.

CHECK IT OUT

American Society for Horticultural Science
600 Cameron Street
Alexandria, Virginia 22314-2562
http://www.ashs.org

American Society of Agronomy
677 South Segoe Road
Madison, Wisconsin 53711
http://www.agronomy.org

Botanical Society of America
1735 Neil Avenue
Columbus, Ohio 43210-1293
http://www.botany.org/bsa

Herb Research Foundation
1007 Pearl Street, Suite 200
Boulder, Colorado 80302
http://www.herbs.org

GET ACQUAINTED

Mindy Green,
Botanist

CAREER PATH

CHILDHOOD ASPIRATION: To be a nurse or teacher.

FIRST JOB: Working afternoons in a grammar school office as part of a high school distributive education assignment.

CURRENT JOB: Author, consultant, and director of education services for the Herb Research Foundation.

STUMBLING INTO A CAREER

Mindy Green started thinking about a career in health when she was in high school. The obvious choice was to become a physical education teacher. She liked to exercise, had danced all her life, and was pretty active in sports, so it seemed like a good fit for her. The problem was that she knew she'd have to take a lot of science classes in order to get a health degree. Since her previous experience with science had not been particularly pleasant, she was scared to commit herself to anything that involved science.

Instead of going to college, Green started working in a health food store in northern California. There she discovered a real interest in diet and nutrition as well as a self-described "hippie" lifestyle, leading her to become more interested in following her heart than in making money. This early experience marks the point from which she began her quest for knowledge about herbs.

NATURAL CAREER CHOICES

Green's career has taken some interesting twists and turns during nearly 30 years of working with herbs. She and her husband left California for Canada to start their own health food store in British Columbia. There Green began teaching classes and creating an interesting product line of herbal blends and herbal extracts. These products became so popular that she started another business, called the Simpler Botanical Company, to sell them.

All her learning at this point had come from reading books and talking to friends with similar interests. Green says that her best education came from searching for answers to customers' questions at the health food store.

Green's formal education started in 1978 when she earned a bachelor's degree in holistic health science (she got over her fear of science!). A master's degree in health and human services as well as special licenses in massage and aesthetics followed as ways to satisfy her desire to learn about the connection between herbs and healthy living.

Later, when Green moved back to California, she became involved with and eventually bought the California School of Herbal Studies. As co-owner, she had the luxury of hiring teachers whom she wanted to learn from and enjoyed some exceptional educational experiences there.

A NEW CHAPTER

Green is currently director of educational services for the Herb Research Foundation. She is responsible for developing information packets about herbs and related health issues and writing articles for natural food publications. You can find her information packets at the Herb Research Foundation's website (http://www.herbs.org).

In addition to her duties at the foundation, Green also consults with various industries. For instance, one popular skin care company hired her to review their products and sent her to New York City to share her expertise with the editors of 20 well-known health and beauty magazines. Green is also a popular speaker at industry conferences and enjoys hosting "herb walks," in which she takes participants on a walk to identify wild plants that are used for food and medicine.

As if all that doesn't keep her busy enough, Green is also an author and has written books such as *Aromatherapy: A Complete Guide to the Healing Art,* written with Kathi Keville (Freedom, Calif.: Crossing Press, 1995); *Calendula: A Keats Good Herb Guide* (Lincolnwood, Ill.: NTC Publishing, 1998); *Natural Perfumes: Simple, Sensual, Personal Aromatherapy Recipes* (Loveland, Colo.: Interweave Press, 1999); *All About Aromatherapy* (Garden City Park, N.Y.: Avery Publishing, 1999).

IT DIDN'T HURT A BIT

Green has enjoyed a successful and fascinating career. Yet, if there was anything she could do differently now, it would be to conquer her fear of science and get a more formal education in plant science earlier. She's learned things as she needed to and can now delve into the scientific aspects of herbs and aromatherapy with the best of them; however, having witnessed her field's evolution over the years, she can see the benefits of a strong science background and recommends such a background to future botanists and herbalists.

BIRDS OF A FEATHER

Green says that many of the friends she started out with in the herb and natural foods business have gone on to find fame and fortune. Some are entrepreneurs whose businesses have made them millionaires, and others are highly regarded authors and consultants who travel the world sharing their expertise. Back then they struggled to earn a decent living, but they all stayed true to work they believed in and are reaping the benefits of it. Green calls it "following bliss." It's allowed her to make a living and make a difference with plants.

Entomologist

WHAT IS AN ENTOMOLOGIST?

An entomologist studies insects such as butterflies, caterpillars, bees, mosquitoes, cockroaches, flies, and grasshoppers. Insects can be amazing to watch in action. They can also be destructive to crops on farms and a hazard to people and animals.

Entomologists work anywhere you find bugs. Many work for government agencies such as state health departments, while others work at university research centers. Another employer of entomologists is industry, offering work as varied as conducting research on pesticides for a chemical company, developing new ways to control household pests for a manufacturing company, recommending ways to eliminate pesky insects for a consulting firm, or finding new ways to produce organic foods for a farm cooperative.

Even though entomology is by its very nature fairly specialized, there are people who study specific types of insects. For instance, a lepidopterist specializes in butterflies, and an apiculturist raises bees. An ecological entomologist studies how insects get along within their environment and their interaction with other creatures. These are big names for working with such small creatures!

Another interesting way to work with insects is beekeeping. The goal of beekeeping is of course to harvest honey to sell. A beekeeper might work with thousands of bees and

grow certain plants for the bees to feed on just so that their honey will have a certain flavor. Even though they sting, with the proper precautions, bees are pretty safe to raise and always fun to watch.

Working with any of these tiny creatures requires highly specialized knowledge. That's why bug scientists usually earn at least a bachelor's degree in college. People involved in research and other high-level positions must have advanced degrees as well.

Success as an entomologist requires a curious mind and creative thinking skills. Not only do entomologists need to know about bugs, they also need to know about the plants that bugs like to eat. They must also study the connection between insects and other animals, the impact that insects have on people, and the interaction insects have with other insects.

Research is an area in which curiosity and creativity intersect with knowledge. For instance, much work is being done to find alternative methods of insect control on farms. Insects like plants and, if left unchecked, can wreak havoc on a crop.

Traditionally, farmers have used potent chemicals called pesticides to keep insects away from their crops; however, pesticides and people can be a dangerous combination. Scientists are linking some health problems to the pesticides people get from food they eat. Entomologists are working hard to help develop better solutions. One solution is to sic certain kinds of bugs on plant-loving bugs. This is called biological control, and it is how much of today's organic food is being produced. Other exciting research involves studying rain forest bugs to see if they hold cures for cancer and other diseases.

While you are pondering a future life as an entomologist, consider this: Insects outnumber people by 200 million to 1. Choose a career with bugs, and you'll have plenty of company!

TRY IT OUT

NECTAR OF THE GODS

You can attract all kinds of butterflies to your own backyard—and in turn observe their metamorphosis—by planting certain wildflowers and milkweed seeds that are rich in nectar (butterflies' favorite food). Plant nurseries even sell special monarch seed mixes to make this process easy and reliable. Whether your garden fills the corner of your family's backyard or just a flower pot or two, it will provide a front row seat for watching the entire metamorphic process. Watch them grow from eggs to caterpillars to butterflies. For additional tips on how to "grow" a butterfly, visit http://www.butterflies.org.

Another option is to purchase a butterfly-rearing kit, which includes a house, feeding kit, and instructions for care. You can order one from the Nature Store at their website—http://www.thenaturestore.com—or by calling toll free: 877-816-3758. There is a cost for the kit, so check with your parents first.

To chase some "cyber" butterflies, check out the links at http://www.butterflywebsite.com.

Use lots of TLC (tender loving care) when handling butterflies. Never handle a butterfly by its wings as this can fatally injure it. Instead try cupping it between the palms of your hands.

YOU'RE IT!

Some butterfly enthusiasts enjoy tagging butterflies so that the butterflies can be tracked as they migrate to and from Mexico. To find out how you can become involved in a monarch tagging program call 888-TAGGING or send an e-mail request to monarch@falcon.cc.ukans.edu.

UP CLOSE AND PERSONAL

All you need to get acquainted with the bugs in your backyard is a net, a jar and its lid punched with air holes, and a magnifying glass. If you want to get fancy, you can purchase special collection sets at many toy stores. Catch a bug, identify it, and observe it. Keep a journal to write notes and draw sketches. Make sure to release it before too long, so you don't hurt it and so you can observe it on its own turf.

For an ongoing observation project, you might want to invest in an ant farm and watch these most productive of insects do their thing. Ant farms can be purchased at most toy stores.

OUCHLESS BEE WATCHING

If you like bees but don't like getting stung, you can observe life in a beehive from the safety of your computer screen. Go to http://ourworld.compuserve.com/homepages/beekeeping. There you can click on the Honey Bee Dance. For more fun facts about bees, also visit http://www.beekeeping.com/index_us.htm.

CHECK IT OUT

American Entomological Society
1900 Race Street
Philadelphia, Pennsylvania 19013

Entomological Society of America
9301 Annapolis Road
Lanham, Maryland 20706
http://www.entsoc.org

North American Butterfly Association
4 Delaware Road
Morristown, New Jersey 07960
http://www.naba.org

Young Entomologists Society
6907 West Grand River Avenue
Lansing, Michigan 48906

GET ACQUAINTED

John R. Watts,
Entomologist

CAREER PATH

CHILDHOOD ASPIRATION: To work with bugs.

FIRST JOB: Cutting a neighbor's grass.

CURRENT JOB: Curator for the Butterfly and Insect Pavilion.

BEES, BUGS, AND BUTTERFLIES

As curator for the Butterfly and Insect Pavilion, John Watts is responsible for taking care of the butterflies that make the conservatory their home. The pavilion was carefully designed for a realistic rain forest atmosphere. Each day, Watts releases new butterfly specimens from all over the world and watches as they delight visitors of all ages.

Butterflies aren't the only inhabitants of the pavilion. Insect exhibits display all kinds of bugs, and a tide pool showcases aquatic invertebrates. And, if keeping track of all these creatures weren't enough to keep Watts busy, he is in charge of all the humans who staff the pavilion too.

SHAKE HANDS WITH A TARANTULA

A favorite part of the exhibit provides hands-on experience with some of the bigger bugs. Visitors get a rare opportunity to hold a tarantula and let it crawl up their arms. It may sound creepy, but it is very safe. It's a great exercise in courage for people—young and old alike—who usually run at the sight of any bug.

Other exhibits feature bees buzzing about their hives and gathering nectar for honey, giant cockroaches climbing the sides of their aquarium cages, and black widow spiders spinning their own magic webs.

BUG KNOWLEDGE

Watts often gets calls to identify suspicious-looking bugs for all kinds of people, including doctors, farmers, and local businesses. This keeps his job full of variety and keeps him in touch with nature. Recently, someone brought him a can of peas that contained a bug. He was asked to identify the bug for the lawyers in court.

He takes special delight in working with all kinds of insects. Bugs are so diverse that Watts is convinced that he will never know all there is to know about insects. He's sure he will never get bored with his work.

A WONDROUS WORLD

Watts' favorite part of a day's work is watching the faces of children light up as he teaches them about the wonder of this incredible world. He loves to talk about bugs—what they do, where they live, what they like and don't like. He enjoys seeing children come into the conservatory and identify all the different kinds of butterflies that they see. He loves to see them pointing and whispering things like "There's a morpho" or "See that zebra longwing," or "Wow, a paper kite."

In addition to teaching schoolchildren, Watts also trains volunteers to work with insects, butterflies, and tide pool invertebrates. You don't have to be an entomologist to volunteer here. You just have to love bugs!

BUSY AS A BEE

Watts' job keeps him hopping. He rarely has time to just sit and enjoy insects the way he would like. Most of the time he is working with volunteers, filling out forms for the government, and sorting shipments of butterflies and insects that arrive from the far reaches of the globe. To maintain a variety of insects, he must stay in touch with people in many different countries. He has lots of friends in faraway places!

The hardest part of his job is keeping the pavilion in tip-top shape. Given the large number of visitors to the pavilion, it's difficult to keep up on the needed maintenance. Changing plants, keeping habitats clean, and feeding the insects requires time. Since these are not activities that can be done while visitors are there, he and his staff work long hours. Keeping things ecologically realistic and balanced can be quite a challenge.

BE PERSISTENT

Watts' advice to anyone interested in becoming an entomologist is to be persistent. Don't give up in your quest for knowledge about bugs. Become very aware of your surroundings. Observe and note what's happening. Look at the ways that bugs affect your life and the lives of other bugs and animals and plants. Most important, says Watts, is to have fun with all those critters!

TAKE A TRIP!

Farmer

SKILL SET

✔ ANIMALS & NATURE

✔ SCIENCE

✔ COMPUTERS

SHORTCUTS

GO   join a local 4-H club.

READ   *Farming and the Environment: Conserving our World* by Mark Lambert (Chatham, N.Y.: Raintree Steck-Vaughn Publishers, 1993).

TRY   growing an herb garden in your windowsill.

WHAT IS A FARMER?

Almost as long as there have been people needing to eat, there have been farmers growing food to feed them. Farming is one of the oldest human occupations. In fact, the very first industry in the United States was farming, brought here by the earliest settlers.

Traditionally, American farms have been family-run operations. Whether comprising a few dozen acres or several

thousand, these farms often provided a living for several generations in the same family. Today, these types of farms are sometimes being replaced by large corporate farms that use expensive state-of-the-art technology, which dramatically increases the productivity of the land.

However, many small farmers have remained competitive by employing some interesting new twists on farming. Some small farmers are banding together into farm cooperatives that allow them to compete with the big guys. Others are starting to cultivate exotic new products such as spices, organic foods, and ostrich meat. These types of products often sell at a higher price, making it easier for small farmers to make a profit. Another strategy is to diversify their operations to produce several similar products that use the same basic equipment and technology. For instance, cattle and buffalo may be raised together, or sugar beets and potatoes might be planted in neighboring fields.

Dairy farming is another huge industry. In the United States, there are more than 22,000 dairy farmers processing more than 32 billion pounds of milk annually. Dairy farming has come a long way from the days when a farmer sat on a stool and hand-milked each cow. It is now a very sophisticated process that can be profitable for small to medium-sized farms.

Farming isn't limited to plants and animals that can be raised on land. Oceans, lakes, and even human-made ponds and hatcheries yield rich harvests in products such as oysters, catfish, shrimp, lobsters, and crab. This type of farming is called aquaculture. Aquacultural farmers actually raise these products from eggs to full-size sea creatures. Unlike fishermen who catch fish in the wild, these farmers raise their crops in controlled environments.

Other types of farms include crop farms on which grain, fruit, vegetables, cotton, and other fiber products are grown. Crop farmers plan, plant, till, fertilize, cultivate, and harvest their crops, as well taking care of pest management. Sometimes they also package and get their products ready for market.

Livestock and poultry farmers raise meat animals on ranches. They feed the animals, keep pens and barns clean and disease-free, supervise breeding programs, and take their animals to market.

Horticultural specialty farms are where flowers, sod, greenhouse fruits and vegetables, and ornamental plants and trees are grown. Some of these crops take several years to get from seedlings to market.

In the operation of all types of modern farms computers play a big part. They are used to keep track of breeding, feeding, and markets for the finished product. Computers are used to monitor the animal feeding process, including the type of feed given to animals, the mix and quality, and the amount. They also help farmers keep in touch with other farmers and stay current on the latest farming information. Computers have become so key to a farm's success that modern farmers often wonder how their predecessors farmed without them.

In many large agricultural areas, processing plants for the products raised in the area will provide additional career opportunities for farmers. These types of companies package fruits and vegetables for supermarkets, grind wheat into flour, press canola seeds into oil, process raw milk for delivery, and much more.

While no formal education is officially required to farm, farming has become so sophisticated that earning a four-year college degree in agronomy or farm management can prove a good investment. In these types of programs, future farmers learn about such issues as pest control, breeding programs and animal husbandry, soil preservation and water quality, meteorology and climatology, and the latest techniques for running a successful farm.

Farming is much more than sticking some seeds in the ground and hoping something grows. It is a complicated business operation. Farming requires hard physical work and diligence. Animals and crops don't take vacations, so time off during peak seasons is rare. There is also a constant struggle to beat Mother Nature at her own game. Too much rain, too little rain, or a bad batch of bugs can all spell disaster for a farmer's livelihood. But, if you are cut out for farming, you'll know it, and nothing will give you as much satisfaction as a well-run farm of your own.

TRY IT OUT

GREEN-THUMB IT!

There's nothing like growing a garden to test your potential as a farmer. Ask your parents if you can adopt a corner of your backyard. Do your homework and figure out what you want to grow before you start digging. Think about what vegetables you like to eat and find out what types of plants grow best in your area. Draw your plan on paper first.

Once you're ready, get the soil ready. First, prepare the soil by turning it over with a shovel, rake it smooth, then make several rows for your seeds. Plant your seeds in rows according to the directions on the back of the seed packages. It will be an ongoing fight to keep the weeds out and to make sure your garden gets enough water and sunlight. Take good care of it and enjoy a big garden party to enjoy the fruits (and vegetables) of your labor.

If you don't have a backyard, start small with a few pots on your windowsill or in a windowbox, or check to see if your town has a community garden that you can share.

WEATHER WATCHER

Weather can be a farmer's best friend—or worst enemy. Start noticing weather trends in your area by keeping a daily log. Each day note the temperature, cloud conditions, rainfall, and wind.

For extra fun, use a farmer's almanac to compare actual weather conditions with those that were predicted by the experts. A good one to consult is the *Old Farmer's Almanac*. This resource has been helping American farmers for more than 200 years; a new edition is published annually by Yankee Books.

GENERAL, PRESIDENT, AND FARMER TOO

First and foremost, George Washington was a farmer, successfully pioneering innovative practices. "Cyber-travel" back in time to President Washington's stately plantation at Mount Vernon and see if you can solve some of his tough farming problems at http://www.mountvernon.org/pioneer/.

CULTIVATE SOME WEBSITES

There are thousands of websites that can give you more information about farming. Here are a few suggestions to get you started.

- ✿ For general information with lots of links, go to Farmer's Guide (http://www.rural.org/Farmers_Guide/Agriculture/Hot_Site.htm).
- ✿ Enjoy some farming fun and games at Kids World (http://www.agr.state.nc.us/cyber/kidswrld) and Kellogg's Planet K (http://www.kelloggs.com).
- ✿ Get the scoop on the fast-growing catfish farming industry at The Catfish Institute (http://www.catfishinstitute.com).
- ✿ View pictures of cows at (http://www. accsyst.com/cow.html). Another cow-related site is the Dairy Farmers of America (http://www.dfamilk.com).
- ✿ Check out the Pokanoket Ostrich Farm (http://www.pokanoket.com/about.htm).

CHECK IT OUT

American Farm Bureau Federation
225 Touhy Avenue
Park Ridge, Illinois 60068
http://www.fb.com

American Society of Agronomy
677 South Segoe Road
Madison, Wisconsin 53711-1086
http://wwwdev.asa-cssa-sssa.org

American Society of Farm Managers and Rural Appraisers
950 South Cherry Street, Suite 508
Denver, Colorado 80222
http://www.agri-associations.org/asfmra

Food and Agricultural Careers for Tomorrow
Purdue University
1140 Agricultural Administration Building
West Lafayette, Indiana 47907-1140

Future Farmers of America
6060 Future Farmers of America Drive
P.O. Box 68960
Indianapolis, Indiana 46268-0960
http://www.ffa.org

National Council of Farmer Cooperatives
50 F Street NW, Suite 900
Washington, D.C. 20001
http://www.ncfc.org

GET ACQUAINTED

Robert Julian Allen III,
Farmer

CAREER PATH

CHILDHOOD ASPIRATION: To have a career in which he could build things.

FIRST JOB: Tractor driver for a general contractor at $1.55 per hour.

CURRENT JOB: Chairman of the board, SouthFresh Farms, a firm that raises catfish.

THE WAVE OF THE FUTURE

Julian Allen had already started several different companies before he began SouthFresh Farms. With SouthFresh, Allen recognized that catfish's time had come because people were in the market for healthier meats. More than 550 million pounds of catfish are produced in the United States. SouthFresh sells its fresh and frozen catfish all over the United States and in Europe.

FRESH IS THEIR MIDDLE NAME

The farming process is fascinating. Baby catfish, called fry hatchlings, are raised in ponds on the farm. Here they live in water carefully monitored to keep it clean and free from chemicals and diseases. They are fed a special blend of soybean meal, corn, and protein. Visitors and workers must meet certain hygiene and disinfectant standards before they can enter the farm.

The fish are seined (gathered into a large net), placed live in special tanker trucks, and taken to the processing plant. Here they are graded for size, shape, and color, cleaned, quick-frozen, and packaged. The time from pond to package is only two hours. That's fresh! (If you want to learn more about this process, check out the company's website at http://www.southfresh.com.)

INVISIBLE INVENTORY

Like most businesspeople starting a new business, Allen needed a loan from the bank in order to buy all the equipment required to get going. Bankers like to know what they are investing in, but that posed a problem for Allen. All his inventory is underwater where bankers can't see it without scuba gear.

Somehow Allen managed to talk his way into a loan that helped him get started. His original 320 acres of ponds "planted" with catfish has grown into 1,600 acres.

LAWN MOWERS AND LUNCH

Allen has learned a few interesting tricks to keep his business swimming along. Early on, he was having some trouble getting the fish's attention at feeding time. He discovered that if he put an old lawn mower (with its blades taken out) on the hill by the pond and turned it on, the fish would swim right over. It was like training a dog (another career Allen considered, but that's another story).

START NOW!

Allen has two words of advice for future farmers: Start now! He suggests that if you want to be a farmer, get involved with your local 4-H or Future Farmers of America clubs. Another option is to start working on a farm as soon as you are old enough, just to get an idea of what goes on there. Start now in developing a good work ethic, which means getting to work on time, working hard, and learning all you can while you do your job.

Hydrologist

SKILL SET

✔ ANIMALS & NATURE

✔ SCIENCE

✔ MATH

WHAT IS A HYDROLOGIST?

A hydrologist studies and protects the water we drink, swim in, and flush. Water is the primary tool of the hydrologist's trade, whether it comes from rivers, lakes, seas, or oceans. A hydrologist, for example, might monitor the flow of a river, its speed, density, and volume. This information helps them make realistic plans for dealing with dams, water levels, and any related water emergencies. Another example might involve a hydrologist monitoring groundwater and ensuring that nothing hazardous seeps into water supplies. Any situation that involves large bodies of water and humans might involve a hydrologist in some way.

Often hydrologists associate with other scientists such as aquatic biologists, geologists, environmental chemists, and wastewater treatment managers. As a team, these experts study water problems, examine their effects on people and other living things, and work out solutions. Their teamwork helps keep our rivers, lakes, and streams pure and safe.

The biggest employer of hydrologists is the federal government in agencies such as the National Oceanic and Atmospheric Administration, the United States Army Corps of Engineers, or the United States Geological Survey (USGS). Universities also hire hydrologists to conduct research and teach. Engineering firms that build treatment plants, levees, canals, dams, and other water-related projects also hire hydrologists. City governments and farming cooperatives employ these experts to monitor drinking water quality and farm wastewater. Power companies that get energy from dams and waterways also employ hydrologists.

Educational requirements vary according to responsibilities. An associate's degree is sufficient to become certified in water and/or wastewater technology. While most states require that wastewater treatment managers pass special tests, on-the-job training is a good teacher in many of these wastewater-related occupations. However, full-fledged hydrologists generally must complete a four-year degree in hydrology, engineering, or another related subject.

Success in this field requires strong computer, math, and science skills. Keen observation skills and the ability to analyze complex situations also come in pretty handy. The end result of a hydrologist's work is good water. Everyone's quality of life is improved with hydrologists on the job.

TRY IT OUT

GLUB, GLUB

How fast does water penetrate the soil around you? Is there more water during some months of the year than others? Do this simple experiment to find out.

First, dig a hole about 6 inches deep in a place that you can observe for several weeks. Second, take a plastic milk bottle, punch lots of small holes in the sides, and cut off the top so you can see inside the bottle and fit a ruler in it. Next, place the bottle in the hole you have dug. Also place another bottle nearby on top of the ground.

Now, keep track of how much water accumulates in each bottle at various intervals and record the results in a small notebook. Do it at the same time each day for several days in a row and record the results.

Do you get the same amount of water in the buried bottle as you do in the bottle on top of the ground? Find out why the levels may be different. The Southeast River Forecast Center (http://www.srh.dnr.state.mo.us/kids.htm) can give you on-line information on water infiltration and percolation.

TRADE CARDS

Learn about dams, the Ice Age, rivers, springs, and other sources of water at the Missouri Department of Natural Resources' website: http://www.dhr.state.mo.us/kids.htm. For a small fee, you can collect trading cards and play water games at the same time.

WATER WEBS

Surf some of these websites for more information on water, hydrologists, and the environment.

- Great Lakes Careers at http://www.schoolship.org/careers/hydrologist.html
- U.S. Geological Survey at http://water.usgs.gov

☿ Great Lakes Information Network at http://www.great-lakes.net/envt/water/hydro.html
☿ Water Science Picture Gallery at http://wwwga.usgs.gov/edu/pictureshtml/divitt.html

CHECK IT OUT

American Institute of Hydrology
2499 Rice Street, Suite 135
St. Paul, Minnesota 55113-3724
http://www.aihydro.org

American Water Resources Association
950 Herndon Parkway, Suite 300
Herndon, Virginia 20170-5531
http://www.awra.org

American Water Works Association
6666 West Quincy
Denver, Colorado 80235
http://www.awwa.org

Association of Ground Water Scientists and Engineers
6375 Riverside Drive
Dublin, Ohio 43017

National Oceanic and Atmospheric Administration
United States Department of Commerce
14th Street and Constitution Avenue NW, Room 6013
Washington, D.C. 20230
http://www.noaa.gov

United States Geological Survey
Water Resources Division
Denver Federal Center, Building 53
P.O. Box 25046, Mail Stop 406
Denver, Colorado 80225
http://www.usgs.gov

GET ACQUAINTED

Douglas Boyer,
Hydrologist

CHILDHOOD ASPIRATION: To be a forest ranger.

FIRST JOB: Working in a grocery store sorting bottles for recycling.

CURRENT JOB: Research hydrologist working for Appalachian Farming Systems Research Center.

WATER CAVEMAN

As part of his job, Douglas Boyer often descends deep into the caves of the Appalachian Mountains to take water samples and look at the hydrology of the caves' ecosystems. He also spends time above and below ground researching aquifers, the water that flows underground, and studying the impact farm animals have on the water.

He also monitors surface mine hydrology, which means he checks out quarry water holes. Often old mines leave pollutants in the water that collect and could run into freshwater systems if left unchecked.

ALL IN A DAY'S WORK

Boyer's work can be physically demanding. Sometimes he has to hike in steep terrain or do some mountain climbing to get his job done. Other times he has to descend into dark caves using ropes to keep himself and his technicians safe. Among his least favorite situations are those in which he must stand in cold water for long periods of time, monitoring and measuring various water sources. In spite of all the challenges,

Boyer says he loves his work because it keeps him outside and in touch with nature.

SOME DAYS ARE LIKE THAT

As with most jobs, Boyer finds that he has good days and bad days. The good ones are when he is outside doing some of the mountain climbing and cave exploring that keep the work so exciting. He also enjoys a good day with other hydrologists as he travels around his territory, sharing stories and common problems. Any day when he can help farmers or miners by giving them the facts about their water quality is also a good one.

Other days are not so much fun. These are the days when Boyer is stuck inside his office doing paperwork or working in the lab. Going to meetings and writing research reports also rank low on his list of favorite things to do. It comes with the territory, though, so Boyer toughs it out while looking forward to getting back outside.

WEATHER WATCHER

Growing up, Boyer was always interested in weather conditions and the outdoors. He especially enjoyed mountain climatology (the study of how weather conditions change in the mountains). He looked at rainfall and soil and water conditions and soon realized the impact these things have on our water supply system. It was great preparation for the work he does now.

RUBBER BOOTS, WADERS, AND COMPUTERS

Boyer's job involves much more than putting on rubber boots and waders to collect water samples. He has to use some very technical knowledge to analyze what he's found and apply sound reasoning to come up with recommendations. To do the kind of work that Boyer does you have to be good in math, strong in computer skills, and well educated in earth science. Boyer encourages anyone hoping to make a career in hydrology to start working on these skills now.

Land Surveyor

SHORTCUTS

SKILL SET

✔ ANIMALS & NATURE

✔ MATH

✔ WRITING

GO find the map for your neighborhood at your local county or city government agency where deeds are recorded.

READ *Pathfinder: A First Guide to Mapping* by Roger Wassell-Smith (Hauppauge, N.Y.: Barrons, 1997).

TRY taking an on-line trip through the history of land surveying at http://www. sligerassociates.com. Click on the history icon to find out how the Egyptians surveyed the land for the pyramids and who the very first registered county surveyor in America was. You'll be surprised!

WHAT IS A LAND SURVEYOR?

Hang on to your hats for this definition of land surveying: Professional land surveying is the application of the rules of evidence, boundary laws, and principles of mathematics and the related physical and applied sciences for measuring and locating lines, angles, elevations, and natural and human-made features in the air, on the surface of the earth, and within underground workings on the beds of bodies of water.

Got all that? Just in case you didn't, here is a simpler version. Land surveyors use what they know about math, science, and history to figure out property boundaries.

Land surveying is actually a very old profession. It makes sense when you consider that people have worked, fought, and died for the ownership of land for as long as anyone can remember. Knowing where your property ends and someone else's begins has always been a key element in civilization. Today, when an acre of prime real estate can be worth millions of dollars, keeping boundary lines straight is pretty important.

While the ancient Egyptians used rope to survey the land where the Pyramids were built, modern surveyors use increasingly sophisticated equipment, such as electronic total stations, data collectors, and handheld computers. Today's surveyors also have another edge over early surveyors: They can now rely on satellites above Earth to help locate places to within one inch of accuracy. This technology, which became widely available after the Persian Gulf War in 1991 is the Global Positioning System (GPS), a combination of satellites and receivers that collects information in order to pinpoint precise positions. It's pretty amazing!

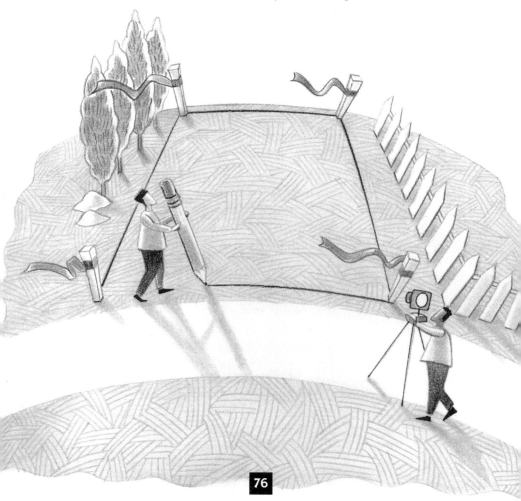

Land Surveyor

Land surveying takes special skills as well as special equipment. A solid math background, especially in geometry and trigonometry, is probably the most important. A surveyor must also be familiar with the history of the land being surveyed in order to walk in the footsteps of the original surveyor. In addition, land surveyors must be able to effectively communicate their findings in written reports.

Surveyors take measurements, draw boundary lines on the ground, and then draw them on maps of the area being surveyed. Surveys are usually required when a new building is being built, when a large piece of land is being developed into smaller lots, when a fence is being built between two neighbors, and when a property owner wants to add to an existing building or thinks someone has erected a building on their land without permission.

Surveyors spend much of their time outdoors, whether in the middle of the city or the heart of a wilderness area. They are often the first ones on a site, before any buildings are constructed, and see it in its rawest or most pristine state. It can be physically demanding work, especially when the weather turns bad.

Surveyors must be licensed in order to conduct surveys that are considered legally binding. In order to become licensed, surveyors must have a combination of six years of training and field experience and they must pass a 16-hour exam. Training usually consists of earning a two- to four-year college degree in any number of subjects, such as math or engineering. Field experience can be earned as part of a field crew working under a licensed surveyor.

Private companies such as engineering, construction, oil and gas extraction, and architectural firms and public utility companies are the biggest employers of land surveyors. Major federal government employers include the United States Geological Survey, the Bureau of Land Management, the Army Corps of Engineers, the Forest Service, the National Oceanic and Atmospheric Administration, and the National Imagery and Mapping Agency. State and local governments provide jobs in highway and urban planning departments and redevelopment agencies. Government tasks include working on roadway and highway designs, water and sewer and septic system layouts, municipal infrastructure, and land development. Even the bike and hiking trails running through parks require a surveyor to lay them out. Some specialty surveyors also lay out underground mines or establish the air space over an airport, while marine surveyors map harbors, rivers, and oceans.

If you become a land surveyor, you'll join the ranks of other famous Americans, such as George Washington, Thomas Jefferson, and Abraham Lincoln, who made important contributions to the surveying profession. Who knows? Maybe you'll even prevent a war or two (or at least a neighborhood feud) over who owns what.

TRY IT OUT

DRAW THE LINE
Take a notebook and walk around your family's yard or a nearby park. See if you can determine the boundaries. Use a tape measure to find out how big the property is and sketch out the dimensions in your notebook by scale (for instance, 1 inch equals 10 yards of land). Sketch the lines and angles of the buildings to get a reasonable facsimile of their design. This is a very simplified version of the mathematical process of land surveying.

Now walk around again and take note of any natural landmarks (the apple tree in the southeast corner, for example) or other distinctive features (such as the neighbor's fence) that make the area surrounding it unique. This is part of recording the history of a place. Both kinds of information would be included in a land surveyor's report and relied on for accuracy in future surveys.

CHARTED TERRITORY
Go to your local library and find a map that represents what an area, such as the present-day site of your school, was like

at least 100 years ago. Get another map that shows what the same area is like now. Make copies of both maps.

Now compare the two. How has it changed in the last 100 years? Use a pencil or highlighter in one color to mark the roads and other landmarks that are the same on both maps. Use another color pencil or highlighter to mark features that are different.

TAKE A WALK ON THE WILD SIDE

Take a walk in the woods with your compass to see what you can learn about direction. Use a field map to follow a path. Each time the path changes direction, write down the new compass heading. Does it go from north to northwest? How many times does it change? Is the path fairly straight or does it change directions frequently? Keep careful notes so that you can put your map away and use only your compass to find your way back.

Maps 101

Thanks to the ingenuity of the United States Geological Survey, you can become an expert on mapmaking and map reading via the Internet. Find your way to the Exploring Maps website at http://www.usgs.gov/education/learnweb/Maps. html. Work your way through activities on location, navigation, information, and exploration.

ON THE WEB

To find out more about land surveying, peruse some of the following interesting websites.

- ☼ Good general association links can be found at Point of Beginning Online (http://www.pobonline.com/association.htm).
- ☼ Virtual Earth tours start at the Land Surveying Info website (http://virtual.er.usgs.gov).
- ☼ Information about marine surveying is available from the National Association of Marine Surveyors (http://www. namsurveyors.org).
- ☼ There's even a place for out-of-this-world surveying at Starlink (http://www.starlinkdgps.com).

CHECK IT OUT

American Congress on Surveying and Mapping
5410 Grosvenor Lane, Suite 100
Bethesda, Maryland 20814-2144
http://www.survmap.org

Council of Professional Surveyors
1015 15th Street NW
Washington, D.C. 20005

Management Association for Private Photogrammetric Surveyors
1760 Reston Parkway, Suite 515
Reston, Virginia 20190
http://www.mapps.org

National Council of Examiners for Engineering and Surveying
P.O. Box 1686
Clemson, South Carolina 29633-1686
http://www.ncees.org

National Geodetic Survey
Information Services
1315 East-West Highway
Silver Spring, Maryland 20910
http://www.ngs.noaa.gov

National Imagery and Mapping Agency
Bobbittral Help Desk (CODH/J-52)
3200 South Second Street
St. Louis, Missouri 63118-3399

National Society of Professional Surveyors
5410 Grosvenor Lane, Suite 210
Bethesda, Maryland 20814

United States Geological Survey Headquarters
12201 Sunrise Valley Drive
Reston, Virginia 20192
http://www.usgs.gov

GET ACQUAINTED

Gene Bobbitt,
Land Surveyor

CAREER PATH

CHILDHOOD ASPIRATION: To be an airline pilot.

FIRST JOB: Working on his family's tobacco farm, later becoming the foreman.

CURRENT JOB: President of Bobbitt Surveying, a land surveying firm in North Carolina.

DRAW THE LINE

Gene Bobbitt spends most of his days marking boundaries for a variety of clients, such as construction companies, developers, and individual homeowners. He covers two states and does both urban and rural work. All of the real work is done outside, in the field. He and his team go in and mark off the boundary lines for a piece of property using complex technical equipment, computers, and satellites, as well as the basic mathematical principles and concepts used by the earliest surveyors.

After compiling all the complex data, Bobbitt goes back to his office and uses his computer to prepare a report. By the time he is finished, he is physically and mentally drained. The work is challenging, demanding, and exciting.

FAMILY FEUD

Sometimes the people involved in a property issue don't agree. For instance, two neighbors might tell him two completely different stories about where their property ends. Things can get pretty hostile especially after he compiles all the facts and does all the measurements and has to tell people that land they thought belonged to them actually belongs to their neighbors. He often gets yelled at in situations like these, but luckily this doesn't happen too frequently.

MAMA MADE ME

When asked why he became a land surveyor, Bobbitt answers honestly by saying "my mama made me." He was just out of college and in his first job as a pharmaceutical researcher, but he was stuck indoors all day. Since he was raised on a tobacco farm, working with horses, other animals, and plants, he'd learned to like working outside. His mother, seeing his problem, linked him up with a friend who was a land surveyor. He hired Bobbitt to cut bushes and forest undergrowth away so the boundaries could be marked. He's been in the profession ever since and has often been glad that he was blessed with such a smart mother.

ON-THE-JOB COMPANIONS

Trees aren't the only obstacles to conducting a land survey in an undeveloped area. There are ticks, foxes, opossum, deer, lizards, groundhogs, raccoons, and other animals to contend with. Snakes are a regular, daily occurrence in Bobbitt's part of the country. It's a good thing that Bobbitt likes working outdoors so much!

In his line of work, Bobbitt gets to meet all kinds of people every day. He also encounters new challenges with each piece of property that he investigates. The people and the variety guarantee that this job is never boring or dull.

FREE TO GET THE JOB DONE

The very best part of this job, according to Bobbitt, is the freedom. Much of the work is done outdoors. There's no one looking over your shoulder, telling you what to do. You just do the best job you can do and hand in the results. Bobbitt finds a lot more pleasure being outside than he would sitting in an office.

ANGLES AND TRIANGLES

Geometry and trigonometry, the areas of math you *really* need to do this job, were Bobbitt's worst subjects in school. When he started on his career, he had some serious catching up to do. He had majored in history and English, which helped in writing reports, but there was no way to get around using tons of math.

Because he works on the East Coast where the first colonists settled, he sometimes sees some interesting original boundary descriptions. For instance, "Start where John saw the bear and go east as far as a horse can ride in one day, then go north to where two streams meet . . ." Those instructions have to be translated into modern terms that everyone can agree on. After all, who will remember where John saw the bear 400 years later? John didn't leave footprints, but Bobbitt does—surveyor footprints.

Bobbit's suggestion to you is to learn the math now. Be willing to work hard and get your hands dirty (even if you don't come across snakes every day). He got started clearing brush along the lines and can't think of a better way for you to get started in the profession. It's fun and you learn a lot!

Marine Biologist

WHAT IS A MARINE BIOLOGIST?

Deep in the ocean lurk such monsters as pollution, food crises and the threat of species' extinction. From giant whales and great white sharks to tiny microbes living in a tide pool, there is a vast diversity of life in our oceans and lakes. Plants and fish need clean water to survive, and ever-increasing numbers of people living near bodies of water are affecting water quality.

Marine biologists study and research the answers to these problems as well as other water issues. Some marine biologists work with dolphins and whales; in fact, that's why a lot of people enter this field. Yet working with dolphins and whales is just a very small part of what marine biology is all about.

Other areas of study that engage marine biologists include the behaviors of sea lions and seals, the ways sharks hunt their food, the secrets of kelp forests, and the mysteries of coral reefs.

Being a marine biologist is more a lifestyle than a job. Diving, working long hours in a laboratory doing research, living at the bottom of the sea, watching the ocean from a submersible observation deck, or swimming with turtles can involve 100 percent of a marine biologist's focus. While a marine biologist often works traditional hours, sometimes a day on the job can involve sitting in a wet bathing suit watching tiny creatures move across the bottom of a tide pool or spending the afternoon floating over a coral reef to observe underwater activity. Not exactly a typical day in the office.

Many marine biologists find work in research at a university or college. Others are employed at aquariums and museums

to help maintain the ecological balance and health of the exhibits. Oil companies also use marine biologists in their ocean drilling operations. Many chemical companies employ marine biologists to develop new drugs and other natural products using various marine organisms. Fishing vessels and seafood packing plants hire these scientists to help with conservation efforts. In addition, the federal government and various state and local governmental agencies also provide a large number of job opportunities for marine biologists.

Of course, the number-one requirement for becoming a marine biologist is a love of water. It's pretty helpful to be a good swimmer, since you'll probably be spending some time underwater during your career. As is true of any type of scientific profession, a marine biologist needs a strong background in math and science and usually at least a bachelor's degree in biology, marine biology, or a related area. A marine biologist involved in research projects must have an advanced degree as well. It's a profession in which learning never really ends because exploration and discovery are key ingredients of any job in marine biology.

TRY IT OUT

UNDERWATER RESEARCH

Before you commit yourself to a career "working with dolphins," make sure that you find out all the facts about this fascinating profession. Here are some books to look for at the library.

Careers in Oceanography and Marine-Related Fields: A Special Edition with Emphasis on Opportunities for Sensory or Physically Disabled Persons. Virginia Beach, Va.: Oceanography Society, 1990.

Potter, Jean. *Science in Seconds at the Beach.* New York: John Wiley & Sons, 1998.

For extensive lists of other interesting books to read, look at the lists supplied by Sea Challengers (http://www.seachallengers.com) and the Society for Marine Mammalogy (http://pegasus.cc.ucf.edu/~smm/strat.htm).

Great information about all kinds of water-related careers can be found at Careers and Jobs in Marine Biology and Oceanography (http://www-marine.stanford.edu/HMSweb/careers.html). Find all kinds of info about marine science at the Virginia Institute of Marine Science website at http://www.vims.edu/adv/ed/careers.

For those willing to invest a few bucks in their future, Woods Hole Oceanographic Institution publishes a wonderful resource called *Marine Science Careers: A Sea Grant Guide to Ocean Opportunities.* To get information or to order a copy, write to Woods Hole Oceanographic Institution, Communications Department, 193 Oyster Pond Road, CRL 209, Woods Hole, Massachusetts 02543-1525, or visit Woods Hole's website at http://www.whoi.edu.

ON-LINE EXPLORATION
Two especially interesting websites concerning marine biology and sea life are the Marine Biology Web (http://life.bio.sunysb.edu/marinebio/mbweb.html) and the aforementioned Society for Marine Mammalogy (http://pegasus.cc.ucf.edu/~smm).

VIRTUAL CRUISE
You don't need a boat to take a leisurely cruise among the Great Lakes. Log on to the Internet to visit the Great Lakes Ecosystem Atlas and conduct some scientific experiments at http://www.uoguelph.ca/zoology/great_lakes/great_lakes.htm.

KING NEPTUNE RULES
What is the largest and deepest body of water on the planet? What is the longest river? Play around in Neptune's Web at http://www.cnmoc.navy.mil/educate/neptune/neptune.htm to find out all kinds of fun facts about Earth's water system.

SAVE YOUR PENNIES FOR CAMP

Make the ocean your classroom at one of the highly regarded SEACAMP programs. Based in California and Hawaii, SEA-CAMP provides marine science education for 7th- to 12th-grade students. These week-long summer camp programs include an invigorating mix of labs, workshops, and research projects, as well as plenty of opportunities for exploring tide pools, scuba diving, taking field trips on research vessels, and more. It's not cheap but is worth every penny if you're looking for a well-rounded introduction to life at sea. Call 800-SEA-CAMP or visit on-line at http://www.seacamp.com for more information.

CHECK IT OUT

American Society of Mammalogists
Monte L. Bean Life Science Museum
Brigham Young University
Provo, Utah 84602-0200
http://asm.wku.edu

Earthwatch Institute
P.O. Box 9104
Watertown, Massachusetts 02471-9104
http://www.earthwatch.org

International Oceanographic Foundation
4600 Rickenbacker Causeway
Miami, Florida 33149

Marine Educators Association
P.O. Box 51215
Pacific Grove, California 93950

Marine Technology Society
1828 L Street NW, Suite 906
Washington, D.C. 20036

Monterey Bay Whale Watch
P.O. Box 52001

Pacific Grove, California 93950
www.montereybaywhalewatch.com

National Science Foundation
1800 G Street NW
Washington, D.C. 20550
http://www.nsf.gov

Oceanography Society
4052 Timber Ridge Drive
Virginia Beach, Virginia 23455
http://www.tos.org

Scripps Institution of Oceanography
8602 La Jolla Shores Drive
La Jolla, California 92037
http://www.sio.ucsd.edu

GET ACQUAINTED

Mia Tegner,
Marine Biologist

CAREER PATH

CHILDHOOD ASPIRATION: To be a firefighter or an astronomer.

FIRST JOB: Camp counselor teaching sailing, canoeing, and skin diving.

CURRENT JOB: Research marine biologist at Scripps Institution of Oceanography.

KELP!

Mia Tegner spends most of her time investigating the mysteries of kelp forests. (Kelp is a kind of large seaweed.) Discovering what lives in the forest, studying how the plants and animals interact with one another, and exploring the physical environment makes the task very interesting for her. Abalones and sea urchins are two of the many important species in this diverse community. Understanding how they are affected by fishing and climate patterns such as El Niño is part of her ongoing research.

At least once a week, Tegner dives into the forest to take readings and check up on the forest community. Her work provides critical information to managers of nearby shore fisheries and sewage treatment plants.

HERE TODAY, WHERE TOMORROW?

When the sea environment changes, it affects the fish and other organisms living in it. It also affects people. People eat the fish produced by the oceans. People swim at the beaches. People ride boats on the surface. If the environment changes, the quality of life is altered for everyone and everything.

Tegner's research gives government resource managers the facts they need to keep our oceans safe and productive. Whether she is considering the effects of sewage on the kelp populations or the effects of overfishing on abalones, Tegner advises on how to keep the environment safe and make it better.

GIANT EYE IN THE DEEP

Tegner's biggest on-the-job surprise came one day when she was diving about 30 feet deep in the ocean. She looked up to see a giant eye watching what she was doing. It was a 40-foot gray whale swimming right next to her—just keeping an eye on her, so to speak.

Tegner sometimes dives with whales, dolphins, and manta rays and loves the opportunity to watch them in their own world. However, Tegner always does a reality check before each dive and doesn't dive under dangerous conditions, such as in cloudy or rough water.

MATH, MATH, MATH

For Tegner, the hardest part of preparing to become a marine biologist was the math. Statistics, in particular, are a big part of her work. Tegner discovered that you don't do statistics without using a lot of math.

Now that Tegner has a job that requires her to use all kinds of sophisticated computer analysis tools, she is glad she took the time to lay that math foundation. She says that students wanting a career like hers need to take all the math and science classes they can.

THE REWARDS

Meeting the challenge of an ever-changing environment is the biggest reward of Tegner's work. She finds it complex and interesting. With constant change, there is certainly no time to get bored. Every day is a new challenge in better managing the ocean's resources. When it is done right, the payoff is big for everyone.

Merchant Mariner

SHORTCUTS

GO on an overnight canoeing trip with a bunch of friends and a couple of parents.

READ *Floating and Sailing* by Terry J. Jennings (Chatham, N.Y.: Raintree Steck-Vaughn Publishers, 1996).

TRY learning how to tie knots to get ready for the rigors of sea life. For a step-by-step guide to more than 100 useful knots, get *The Handbook of Knots* by Des Pawson (New York: DK Publishing, 1998).

SKILL SET
- ✔ ADVENTURE
- ✔ ANIMALS & NATURE
- ✔ MATH

WHAT IS A MERCHANT MARINER?

A merchant mariner travels the waterways of the world on a boat, ship, ferry—virtually anything that floats—for both commercial and recreational purposes. Transporting cargo accounts for a big part of the world's water traffic. In 1995 alone, a total of 4.687 billion tons of cargo was shipped around the world, including 402 million tons of iron ore, 1.414 billion tons of oil, and 196.2 million tons of grain. It takes a lot of ships to move that much cargo and a lot of people to run those ships.

There are many different ways to earn a living on a ship. The top job is as captain or master. The captain is ultimately responsible for the ship, its contents, and the people onboard. The captain is in command and what he or she says goes—or else. The captain determines the ship's course and must be able to read charts and use other navigational aids. He or she must be an expert in all things related to the ship and must make sure everything stays in good shape.

Other important members of the crew include the following:

Deck officer, or **mate,** who assists the captain. The deck officer makes sure the cargo is secure and supervises the crew and ship activities. This person is second in command and acts as captain whenever necessary.

Engineer, who takes care of the engines and machinery onboard.

Seaman, or **deckhand,** who does the chores needed to keep things running smoothly—swabbing decks, hoisting sails, and other physically demanding tasks.

Pilot, who guides ships in and out of harbors or through small waters where the captain may not be familiar with the local tides, currents, and other hazards.

Mariners keep their ships operating in all kinds of weather, under all sorts of conditions. They spend long periods of time at sea, away from home. Living conditions onboard a ship are often crowded with little privacy.

In addition to the crew, certain kinds of ships may have additional staff onboard. For instance, a luxury cruise ship would have entertainment directors, chefs, lifeguards, and other support people you'd expect to find at a resort. Hospital ships would, of course, have medical personnel onboard.

Almost half of all merchant mariners in the United States work on private merchant marine cargo ships or U.S. Navy Military Sealift Command ships in "bluewater" jobs, working in the open oceans. "Brownwater" jobs on tugboats, ferries, dredges, and other harbor and lake watercraft account for almost as many of the jobs. Other mariners work on cruise ships, medical hospital ships, private yachts, and sightseeing and excursion boats.

Training and licensing requirements are governed by the United States Coast Guard. Anyone who operates a watercraft must be licensed, but licenses vary depending on the size and type of boat. Many must also pass both a written and physical examination and a drug screening. While some of the jobs onboard a ship don't require any formal education, anyone who works onboard a ship that weighs more than 100 tons must have a merchant mariner's license.

To be an officer, you must have education plus work experience. The United States Merchant Marine Academy offers a four-year bachelor of science degree and a license as a deck officer or engineering officer upon graduation. Experience and additional exams are required to move up in rank. Competition for jobs as a merchant mariner can be stiff, so the more schooling you have, the better.

TRY IT OUT

MAROONED!

Imagine yourself stranded on a desert island. What supplies would you most want with you? Make a list of what you would take and why.

Life at sea isn't quite like being marooned, but the space limitations mean sailors have to make some hard choices about what they bring and what they leave behind.

S.O.S

Ships at sea communicate with one another using flags. The Maritime Flag Signalling System was introduced in 1934. It is based on a system of 26 letters and 10 figures and can be "read" no matter what language a ship's crew may speak. To find out more about the language of ships, visit Wordworkers at http://www.wordworkers.nl/flagmain.htm.

SAFE AT SEA

Any good sailor knows to respect the water. Learn the basic water safety rules through Clemson University's Cooperative Extension Service at http://www.cgs.clemson.edu/water_s.htm.

FORE OR AFT?

Before you launch a nautical career, learn the lingo. Get a stack of index cards and go on-line to http://www.refer.fr/termisti/nauterm/dicten.htm#en, the Maritime Terminology site. Here you'll find definitions for words such as *bow, stern, ballast, fathom, hull, knot, port,* and *starboard.* Take the time to learn terms like these now and you'll save yourself some embarrassing blunders when you get onboard a ship.

SAIL THE WEB

Finding your place in the maritime industry can be a challenge. The following websites include a diverse mix of sea-related resources. Investigate where the best careers might be for you by learning all you can about the options.

- ☀ A good site for general information about the American Merchant Marine is http://www.USMM.org.
- ☀ Click into Sea Education Association's website for some seafaring activities at http://www.seaeducation.org/Webmaster/K12Top.htm.
- ☀ Go to the movies on-line with the San Diego Maritime Museum at http://www.sdmaritime.com.
- ☀ Several sites will give you a closer look at tall ships and provide information on summer camp opportunities for kids including:
  http://www.tallshipbounty.org
  http://www.tallshipadventures.com
  http://www.sailingship.com
- ☀ Find out about water safety at http://www.uscgboating.org.

ONBOARD READING
Books are a great way to enjoy a mariner's life from the comfort of dry land. Here are a few that are sure to fascinate.

Boats and Ships. New York: Scholastic, 1996.

Dempsey, Deborah Doane. *The Captain's a Woman: Tales of a Merchant Mariner.* Annapolis, Md.: United States Naval Institute Press, 1997.

Graham, Ian. *Boats, Ships, Submarines, and Other Floating Machines.* New York: Kingfisher Books, 1995.

For a list of other additional reading suggestions, visit Maritime Books, News and Publishers (http://w3.ime.net/~drwebb/logbook.htm) and the Maritime Home Page (http://www.webcom.com/~maritime/homepag3.html).

CHECK IT OUT

American Society of Naval Engineers
1452 Duke Street
Alexandria, Virginia 22314-3458
http://www.navalengineers.org

International Organization of Masters, Mates and Pilots
International Headquarters
700 Maritime Boulevard
Linthicum Heights, Maryland 21090-1941
http://www.bridgedeck.com

Sea Education Association
P.O. Box 6
Woods Hole, Massachusetts 02543
800-552-3633
http://www.seaeducation.org

Society of Naval Architects and Marine Engineers
601 Pavonia Avenue
Jersey City, New Jersey 07306
http://www.sname.org

United States Coast Guard
Licensing and Manning Compliance Division (C-MOC-1)
2100 Second Street SW
Washington, D.C. 20593-0001
http://www.uscg.mil

Woods Hole Oceanographic Institution
Woods Hole, Massachusetts 02543-1050
http://www.whoi.edu

Youth Maritime Training Association
2512 Second Avenue, Room 303
Seattle, Washington 98121
http://www.pacifier.com/~rboggs/YMTA.HTML

GET ACQUAINTED

Peg Brandon,
Merchant Mariner

CAREER PATH

CHILDHOOD ASPIRATION: To sail around the world with Jacques Cousteau.

FIRST JOB: Running a youth employment service for high school students.

CURRENT JOB: Marine super-intendent for Sea Education Association (SEA).

TALL SHIPS

Sailing the ocean in a tall ship, the kind that used to ply the seas in the 1800s, is exciting, beautiful, and peaceful. Peg Brandon captains one of these tall ships, used in the Sea Education Association's education programs. The school has two ships that contain more than 7,000 square feet of sails. One is a 125-foot schooner named the SSV *Westward,* and the other, a 135-foot brigantine called the SSV *Corwith Cramer.*

The ships are used to provide one- to six-week education-al voyages for high school students. While onboard, the students conduct research and a variety of experiments. For instance, they make hydrocasts (deploying sensor collection bottles) and biological tows (plankton nets) and conduct studies on biological assays (estimation of marine virus concentrations), sediment sampling and analysis, and chemical analysis.

Brandon has been with SEA for 12 years and has moved through the ranks to become the marine superintendent, supervising voyages in the north Atlantic Ocean. She didn't set out to become a sea captain, however; she was a science major in college and signed on with SEA to do some research. She got off that first boat with SEA and onto another one right away and has spent most of her life since then involved with large sailing vessels in some way.

Other jobs she has held include working with school kids cleaning up New York City's harbor and rivers, and in Alaska working on a converted mine sweeper (there's very little wind in Alaska, making it difficult for sailing ships to operate). Then she settled back at SEA because she loves the water, sailing, and working with young people.

At sea, she is the captain, responsible for the lives of all 35 people on board and for the safety of a 250-ton ship. On land, she teaches nautical science at the SEA school.

Follow the progress of one of SEA's voyages on its website: http://www.sea.edu.

TEAMWORK

Brandon says that once you take off on an ocean voyage, it's just you and your crew. Your very survival depends on working with one another. You have to call upon what's inside you and always give your best to the effort.

Being in close quarters with a bunch of strangers helps people get acquainted really quickly. Getting along and working together are a big part of the learning experience on Brandon's trips.

PLAN AHEAD

A successful voyage begins long before the ship leaves shore. Planning is one of Brandon's responsibilities. Adequate food, water, medical supplies, and other equipment must be stowed away before the ship leaves port. Carefully planning the route and making sure that the ship is seaworthy are also Brandon's responsibility.

CHALLENGES

Sometimes it isn't easy to anticipate what will happen next. Weather plays a big part in sailing. Although smart captains generally try to avoid severe storms while at sea, sometimes one comes up unexpectedly.

Going through a storm in a tall ship can make for a wild ride. The real work starts when the wind is blowing ferociously, the waves are high, and the rain is coming down so thick you can't see. There are heavy sails to raise and lower, giant anchors to drop and bring up from the bottom of the ocean, and the ship still must be kept clean and in top condition. Brandon says it's scary, but you learn to stretch your limits farther than you thought possible.

SUNRISE ON DAWN WATCH

Dawn watch on a tall ship is one of the biggest perks of the job, according to Brandon. There's nothing quite like the spectacular sights you see in the wee hours between 3:00 and 7:00 A.M. while standing watch on a ship.

Brandon particularly remembers a time when her ship was anchored on Silver Bank in the Caribbean. Land isn't visible, even though the water is very shallow there. It is a spot where humpback whales come to give birth. As they got ready to leave one morning, a mother whale and her new baby came right alongside the ship. They circled and rubbed up against the ship. It was a rare opportunity to see a mother and baby whale at play.

BRING YOUR RAINCOAT

Brandon loves being so close to nature when she's on a ship. But in the rain, sleet, or wind, the only thing between you and the elements is, perhaps, a raincoat. There's no running away from the weather on a ship. You learn to deal with it—and truly appreciate it. There are no barriers or boundaries. This brings some challenges, but more rewards. According to Brandon, it's one of the best parts of being a ship captain.

Park Ranger

WHAT IS A PARK RANGER?

Can you think of anything more pleasant than spending a sunny day in the park? How about devoting your career to working in one? With more than 76 million acres of national park land in the United States, there is plenty of room for park rangers interested in educating and protecting the millions of visitors who enjoy these national treasures. And, while national parks are the obvious choice for park rangers, there are also many state and local park and recreation districts that employ park rangers.

The responsibilities of a park ranger are many and varied. First and foremost, a park ranger is concerned about safety. Ensuring safe parks can involve anything from simply enforcing park rules and regulations to leading daring rescues to find lost or endangered hikers. The safety-related duties of a park ranger are to protect the park from the people, to protect the people from the park, and to protect the people from the people.

Another important part of a park ranger's work is to inform and guide visitors so they make the most of the natural and cultural resources found in each park. To accomplish this, park rangers might guide a nature walk, teach a class, or even share stories about the history of the park. Park rangers who specialize in bringing the past alive through educational experiences are called interpreters.

Forest ranger is a related occupation that is often confused with park ranger. A park ranger works in pristine areas preserved as national or state parks and focuses on protecting natural and historic features and supervising recreational activities. In contrast, a forest ranger works in national forests that are just as likely to be designated for recreation and preservation as they are for lumber harvesting, cattle grazing, and mineral production. Both careers require a love of the outdoors, an appreciation of nature, and a willingness to work with people.

Other closely related but significantly different occupations include conservation officer, game warden, and park security officer. Job titles and duties vary according to the tasks assigned to different government agencies. For instance, someone working for the Bureau of Land Management might be concerned with conserving natural resources in a park while someone working for the U.S. Fish and Wildlife Service might focus on managing endangered species in a national park.

Regardless of the title, a college degree in a program such as forestry, geology, botany, conservation, or wildlife management helps open doors in these competitive fields. In addition, experience working in parks or conservation is a plus. Park rangers with strong communication and administrative skills stand the strongest chance of moving up through the ranks of park management.

Mind you, the work of a park ranger isn't all glorious sunsets and nature hikes. A park ranger works in all kinds of weather and in all kinds of terrain. National parks especially can be located in rather remote areas, making living accommodations rustic. In many cases, working in the park service is as much a calling as it is a vocation. Either park rangers love it and commit themselves fully to their work or they hate it and seek other ways to apply their valuable ranger skills to different jobs. There is, however, a great sense of satisfaction to be found in a job that involves preserving natural and cultural treasures.

TRY IT OUT

THE ARMCHAIR ADVENTURER

Where do you want to go today? Whether it's the Gates of the Arctic National Preserve in Alaska, the Grand Canyon in Arizona, or the Thomas Jefferson Memorial in Washington, D.C., these sights are all as close as a click of a mouse—no matter where you live. To tour a whole country full of wonderful national parks, check out the U.S. National Park Service's website at http://www.nps.gov/parks.html.

While you are there, make a wish list of the top 10 you'd like to visit someday in person. If you get the chance to actually visit any national parks, make sure to find out if they participate in the Junior Ranger Program. This program provides all kinds of exciting ways to learn about national parks. For information about the program, look on the Internet at http://www.nps.gov/interp/jrranger.html.

WORK YOUR WAY TO THE TOP

There's no substitute for on-the-job experience when it comes to understanding the work of a park ranger. Give yourself a few years and think about applying for a volunteer position with the high school–level Conservation Work Crew of the Student Conservation Association (SCA). The program offers short-term employment opportunities in national parks and forests around the country. It's hard work, but it provides great outdoor training and work experience and gives young people a chance to do something tangible to protect our natural resources. For information about the program contact SCA at P.O. Box 550, Charlestown, New Hampshire 03603, or visit their website at http://www.sca-inc.org.

PARK RANGER AT PLAY

If you're going to be a park ranger someday, you've got a lot to learn about things such as water, wetlands, endangered species, and public lands. Get a jump start on the learning process and have some fun with the activities found at the following websites.

- ☼ National Wildlife Federation at http://www.nwf.org/nwf/kids
- ☼ National Park Service at http://www2.cr.nps.gov/pad/adventure/landmark.htm
- ☼ Environmental Protection Agency at http://www.epa.gov/kids
- ☼ Discovery Online at http://www.discovery.com/stories/nature/endangered/endangered.html

Sites related to specific parks that you might enjoy include

☼ Colorado State Parks at http://www.parks.state.co.us/kids
☼ Blue Ridge Parkway at http://www.nps.gov/blri/ kids.htm
☼ Wisconsin Department of Natural Resources at http:// www.dnr.state.wi.us/KidStuff.html
☼ Missouri Department of Natural Resources at http:// www.dnr.state.mo.us/kids/htm

No list of park and forest resources would be complete without an address to visit Smokey Bear. Join him for some fun and games at http://www.smokeybear.com.

KING OF THE JUNGLE

It's not every day you get the chance to create your own park from scratch. SimPark, a software game published by Maxis, gives you that chance. Whether it's a wild and untamed jungle, a lush forest, a breathtaking meadow, or even an unrelenting desert, the game lets you use your imagination. In the process, you'll learn a bit about how various plants and animal species fit into different kinds of ecosystems. You can download a demo version of the game at http://www.gamedemo.com/strategy/simpark/cheats.htm. To obtain a full-fledged version of the game, look at your local software store or order it on-line at http://www.eastore. ea.com/cgi-bin/eastore.storefront.

CHECK IT OUT

American Park Rangers Association
P.O. Box 1348
Homestead, Florida 33090

Association of National Park Rangers
P.O. Box 108
Larned, Kansas 67550
http://www.anpr.org

National Association of State Park Directors
9894 East Holden Place
Tucson, Arizona 85748

National Recreation and Park Association
22377 Belmont Ridge Road
Ashburn, Virginia 20148

Student Conservation Association
P.O. Box 550
Charlestown, New Hampshire 03603
http://www.sca-inc.org

GET ACQUAINTED

Phyllis Yoyetewa,
Park Ranger

CAREER PATH

CHILDHOOD ASPIRATION: To be a teacher or social worker.

FIRST JOB: Working for the National Park Service as a student intern during high school.

CURRENT JOB: Interpretation park ranger at the Grand Canyon National Park.

LIVING IN TWO DIFFERENT WORLDS

Phyllis Yoyetewa is a Native American and grew up in the Grand Canyon village. She is part Apache and part Hopi but was raised with the Hopi beliefs. She learned to speak the Hopi language before she learned English.

She says that growing up as a Native American was sometimes difficult because she felt like she was trying to live in two different worlds. In one world, she treasured the Hopi traditions and learned all the stories so that she could share them with future generations. In the other world, she was trying to get a good education so that she could pursue a career.

Having the Grand Canyon as a playground was an extra special part of Yoyetewa's childhood. She remembers her mother dressing her up and letting her walk around the Hopi house, a popular tourist spot in the Grand Canyon area. Tourists liked to take pictures of the "little Indian girl" and would give her coins to take home. She says that she was always exploring the rim of the Grand Canyon and that a favorite sledding spot was later discovered to be a very important fossil site.

A CHANGE OF PLANS

When Yoyetewa graduated from high school, she went to the Yavapai Junior College with plans to become a social worker. Those plans changed in the wee hours one morning when Yoyetewa and a friend were driving back to school after a visit home. Yoyetewa's friend fell asleep at the wheel of the car, and they had a very bad car accident. Yoyetewa's hand was injured so badly that she was unable to write for two years. Completing college was no longer an option for Yoyetewa.

After recovering from her injuries and giving birth to a daughter, Yoyetewa started working at a bank and later got a job at a Grand Canyon school. Working as a teacher's assistant, she tutored Indian students and taught a special class about different Indian tribes in the United States.

She enjoyed the job, but because it didn't pay much, she had to get another part-time job. She started working as a fee collector for the National Park Service during the summer months and on weekends. The Park Service eventually offered her a full-time position, and she was on her way to becoming a park ranger.

A GIFT OF GAB

For the past several years, Yoyetewa has been working as an interpretation park ranger at the Grand Canyon National

Park. Her responsibilities include giving guided walks and talks and answering visitors' questions. When she was first offered this job, it presented a dilemma. According to Hopi tradition, women don't speak in public. Her family advised her that times are changing and the opportunity would be a good one to help preserve the Hopi legends, so she accepted the position.

Yoyetewa confesses that while it was difficult to get her started speaking to groups of people, now it's hard to get her to shut up! She loves having the chance to share her stories with people from all over the world.

BACK TO SCHOOL

Even though Yoyetewa never got the chance to finish college, this job gives her plenty of chances to learn. It takes lots of homework to learn enough to be able to speak intelligently about something in front of groups of curious tourists. She's had to study a lot about geology—a real challenge since Yoyetewa did not have a science background.

One of the best parts of Yoyetewa's job is sharing stories that have passed down from her Hopi ancestors. Among her favorites is one about the origin of the Grand Canyon. According to Hopi legend, a Hopi grandmother entrusted a pottery jar filled with something very powerful to her young grandson, Pookonghoya. She instructed him to take the jar to the chief of Old Aribi to help him win a battle against enemies who were encroaching on Hopi lands. Although the grandmother had given Pookonghoya strict instructions not to open the jar, his curiosity got the best of him as he neared Desert View, the site of the fierce battle. When he opened the jar there was a big noise and lightning went in three directions. According to legend, that is how the Grand Canyon, the Colorado River, and the Little Colorado River were formed.

DAY AFTER DAY

Yoyetewa gets the chance to tell stories like that every day. She might start a day with a morning nature walk in which she talks about local plants and explains how Native Americans

used them. Then she might lead an afternoon history walk in which she guides a tour of a historic village and talks about the different buildings and customs of early residents of the area. She also spends a great deal of time at the information desk answering tourists' questions and sometimes dispelling myths about her people.

GOOD ADVICE FOR A YOUNG GENERATION

As a Hopi, Yoyetewa feels an obligation to help young Native Americans find their place in life. She often speaks to groups of students and offers this advice.

- ☼ Start figuring out when you are young what you want to do with your life.
- ☼ Study hard from the time you are in kindergarten.
- ☼ Make sure that you get at least two years of college training.
- ☼ Do something for yourself before you start a family.

And most important, Yoyetewa says to aim for the stars and go as high as you can go.

Pet Groomer

SHORTCUTS

SKILL SET

✔ ANIMALS & NATURE

✔ TALKING

✔ BUSINESS

GO to a dog grooming shop to see before and after examples of a groomer's work.

READ all you can about your favorite breeds of dogs or cats.

TRY giving your family (or neighbor's) pet a soothing bath and brushing out its hair.

WHAT IS A PET GROOMER?

Transforming shaggy mutts into adorable pets often sums up what a pet groomer does. Whether it's a tiny teacup poodle or a lovable lug of an Old English sheepdog, animals have bad hair days too and need help to look their best. Some resourceful pet owners take care of pet grooming chores on their own, but others choose to pay a professional pet groomer to do the job instead.

With an estimated 117 million dogs and cats sharing homes with U.S. families, pets account for some big business opportunities. Many of these pet owners think of their pets as members of the family. In fact, 65 percent of pet owners gave their pets a Christmas present, 24 percent celebrate their pets' birthday, and 41 percent have pictures of their pets on display in their homes or offices. Another 30 percent are so concerned about their pets' happiness that they tend to leave the radio or television on so their pets don't get lonely when left alone. Given all this, it's no wonder that many pet owners don't think twice about spending $20 to $50 to get their pets clean and groomed.

Pet grooming can be a lucrative career option for animal lovers. According to one survey, pet groomers report earnings between $30,000 and $100,000 a year and may serve more than 2,000 clients. Some groomers are self-employed and set up space in their homes for their grooming work, while others open pet grooming shops and may employ or rent space to other groomers. Still other groomers may work in association with a veterinarian or as an employee of a full-service pet shop.

Pet grooming involves a variety of processes to keep animals' coats, nails, teeth, and ears in tip-top shape. A typical grooming process might include brushing out a pet's coat, a bathing and drying regimen, clipping and trimming the pet's coat, cleaning the pet's ears and teeth, and clipping nails. Just like stylists who work with people, pet groomers must know all the latest looks and match them to the appropriate breeds of pets. There are literally dozens of very specific "hairstyles" to master. It takes creativity and skill to do it right.

At this time, there are no formal training or licensing requirements for pet groomers; however, there is plenty to

learn before setting up shop. There are two ways to learn the ropes of this profession. One way is to work as an apprentice with an experienced groomer. This method takes a lot of self-discipline and a real commitment to acquire the skills needed to succeed. Plenty of hands-on experience is the key to launching a grooming career via this route.

The other way to become a pet groomer is to attend a special trade school that provides 500 to 600 hours of training and practice in pet grooming skills. Either route also requires ongoing professional development by reading trade journals and attending seminars and conferences to stay up on the latest trends and techniques in the industry.

In addition to grooming, other ways to center a business and career around pets include being a pet-sitter or dog walker or by working in kennels, day camps, and pet shops. Pet-sitters take care of other people's pets while they are on vacation or at work. This may involve simply the basics of walking and feeding the pet a couple times a day or may actually mean staying in the home to take care of the pet's every whim. Kennels are essentially pet hotels and are places where pets stay while their owners are away. Traditionally kennels have meant rows of stark cages and outdoor runs, but cozier, more pet-friendly kennels have recently sprung up all over the country. These offer services that are roughly equivalent to what a person might find at a luxury resort: smartly decorated "suites" with comfortable sleeping accommodations, indoor and outdoor playgrounds, special treats, and other perks to assure that pets enjoy their visits. Along this same line are doggy day camps, which cater to the pets of working people. Pets are dropped off in the morning and enjoy a full day of play and exercise before being picked up in the evening.

As long as people love their pets and as long as those pets get dirty and shaggy and need extra care, there will be plenty of potential customers for the capable pet groomer and caregiver. Animal lovers with a creative bent and an entrepreneurial streak may want to explore putting their talents to good use with pets!

TRY IT OUT

PETS 101

Probably the most useful thing you can do now to prepare for a future pet grooming career is to get to know some of the wonderful breeds of cats and dogs that people adopt as pets. Consider investing in a notebook and some dividers to start keeping track of what you learn. Look for pictures of different kinds of domestic animals in magazines, newspapers, and brochures and glue them onto pages in the notebook. Jot down fun facts that you discover about each breed.

For information about clubs, organizations, and associations that cater to specific kinds of animals check out the Tame Beast's website at http://www.tamebeast.com/12.htm. For breed-specific grooming information, check out the Groomers Lounge at http://www.groomers.com/breeds.

PRETTY PETS, INC.

Owning and operating a shop is the aspiration of many pet groomers. You can get the inside scoop about what it takes to succeed in two resources. The first resource is a book, by Madeline Bright Ogle, entitled *From Problems to Profits: The Madson Management System for Pet Grooming Businesses* (Gardnerville, Nev.: Madson Group, 1997).

The second resource is the PetGroomer.com website (http://www.petgroomer.com). Here you'll find nearly 500 pages of fun pet grooming industry information for both the professional and wanna-be pet groomer.

SETTING UP SHOP

Pet grooming is a relatively inexpensive business to start up. You need space to serve your clients—in your home or in a shop—and some basic supplies. Pretend that you've finished your training and are ready to set up shop. Make a list of the supplies you'll need to get started. For some help and inspiration, consult the resources available at the Groomer's Mall on-line at http://itsnew.com.

For a different twist on this activity, come up with ideas for an extra special pet spa or resort. What kinds of activities and services would you offer to pamper your four-legged clients?

THE WELL-GROOMED PET

Here is a list of books you can use to further your education in pet grooming.

All (87) Breed Dog Grooming for the Beginner. Neptune, N.J.: TFH Publications, 1998.

Francais, Isabelle, and Richard Davis. *All Breed Dog Grooming.* Neptune, N.J.: TFH Publications, 1988.

Pinney, Chris C. *Guide to Home Pet Grooming.* Hauppauge, N.Y.: Barrons Educational Series, 1990.

Ruiz, Suzanne. *A Dog Owner's Guide to Grooming Your Dog.* Blacksburg, Va.: Tetra Press, 1996.

Stone, Ben, and Pearl Stone. *The Stone Guide to Dog Grooming for All Breeds.* Charlottesville, Va.: Howell Book House, 1991.

If the Internet is your preferred source of up-to-the-minute information, look for dog grooming tips at either of these interesting sites:

- ☼ http://www.acmepet.com/canine/groom/article/intro.html
- ☼ http://www.ivillage.com/pets

Put your newfound skills to work by taking good care of your own pets. Taking the time to pamper your pets is a great way to help them feel loved and wanted.

CHECK IT OUT

American Grooming Shop Association
4575 Galley Road, Suite 4001
Colorado Springs, Colorado 80915

American Pet Association
P.O. Box 725065
Atlanta, Georgia 31139
http://www.apapets.com/apapets

Intergroom
250 East 73rd Street
New York, New York 10021
http://www.intergroom.com

International Professional Groomers
1108 West Devon
Elk Grove Village, Illinois 60007

International Society of Canine Cosmetologists
2702 Covington Drive
Garland, Texas 75040

National Dog Groomers Association of America
P.O. Box 101
Clark, Pennsylvania 16113
http://www.nauticom.net/www/ndga

GET ACQUAINTED

Chichie Tascoe,
Pet Groomer

CAREER PATH

CHILDHOOD ASPIRATION: Never thought about anything except working with animals.

FIRST JOB: Pet groomer.

CURRENT JOB: Owner of Chichie's Canine Design and Grooming Spa.

ANIMAL LOVER

There are no two ways about it. Chichie Tascoe loves animals. From the time Tascoe was a very young child, animals were a big part of her life. Many a stray dog and cat found haven in her care. Tascoe says that her interest in animals probably kept her out of a lot of trouble as she was growing up. She was too busy looking after her menagerie of cats, dogs, and other pets, including the occasional monkey.

She never has outgrown her love of animals either, much to her husband's surprise. After she married and had children of her own, there were still animals everywhere. Her kids had a ball looking after an endless procession of dogs, cats, squirrels, raccoons, hamsters, turtles, mice, birds, and snakes.

It seems part of a natural flow that Tascoe found her life's work as a pet groomer. She says it started as a hobby—she was more interested in getting her hands on her friends' dogs than in earning money. She taught herself the basics by looking at pictures and used her own artistic talents to create unique and attractive designs for each pet. Her reputation grew and the hobby soon became a full-fledged business. That was in 1965, and Tascoe has been at it ever since.

HAIL TO THE PUP!

Tascoe is now the owner of a pet grooming shop in Georgetown, a suburb of Washington, D.C. There she tends to some of the capital's most interesting and powerful residents. Among her more famous clients was Leader, the pampered schnauzer belonging to former Kansas senator Bob Dole and his wife, Elizabeth Dole. According to Tascoe, Leader came in about once a month for a water and aromatherapy spa treatment and always acted very dignified, just like his owners.

Tascoe makes a point of knowing each of her canine clients by name, whether they are famous or not. She takes the time to get to know them and to make sure that their experience at her shop is a pleasant one.

MORE THAN A HAIRCUT

A day at Tascoe's shop starts with a calming brush-out. Groomers speak gently to the dogs to calm their jitters. A soothing bath follows with any of a number of special spa treatments. Tascoe makes sure dogs are comfortable while their hair is styled. She and her staff take their time and give the dogs a chance to rest and change positions often during the sometimes lengthy grooming process. No muzzles or nooses allowed!

ALL CREATURES GREAT AND SMALL

Tascoe credits her animal friends for teaching her some of the most valuable lessons she's learned about life. Trust, unconditional love, relying on instincts, and even dying with dignity are things she's learned from her furry friends. She's learned to relax and enjoy life and says that working with animals is a surefire way to conquer stress.

Recycling Entrepreneur

SHORTCUTS

GO visit a composting demonstration site near you.

READ *Earth-Friendly Outdoor Fun: How to Make Fabulous Games, Gardens, and Other Projects from Reusable Objects* by George Pfiffner (New York: John Wiley & Sons, 1996).

TRY recycling your family's trash.

SKILL SET

✔ ANIMALS & NATURE

✔ BUSINESS

✔ COMPUTERS

WHAT IS A RECYCLING ENTREPRENEUR?

An entrepreneur is someone who launches and manages a business venture; therefore, a recycling entrepreneur is some who launches and manages a recycling venture. This type of business venture starts with the old adage that one person's trash is another person's treasure. A recycling entrepreneur finds creative ways to reuse refuse that otherwise would be tossed out and finds ways to build a profitable business around these ideas. Turning old license plates into dust pans, burned-out electric lightbulbs into kerosene lanterns, old tires into playground surfaces—these are the kinds of creative ideas that can make fortunes for a savvy businessperson.

Of course, another great result of recycling is that it helps save natural resources, energy, and landfill space. (Did you know that recycling a glass bottle saves enough energy to light one bulb for four hours?) Eventually we will run out of places to stash our trash. The entrepreneur may make money from recycling, but everyone benefits from it.

Some businesses specialize in recycling itself. For instance, they may provide a recycling pickup service that operates like a trash pickup service, except that the trash is sorted and sold to other businesses that use the materials for new products. Other businesses may process recycled materials to get them ready for reuse. For example, they may prepare old newspapers to make new paper or melt used plastic containers to get them ready for new uses. Other types of businesses specialize in a particular type of recycled product. Glass, metals, paper, petroleum products, plastics, batteries, and chemicals are just a few recyclable materials. Even old computers get recycled.

An entrepreneur is someone with a good idea who does the work to make it succeed. In business, as in most things in life, the difference between success and failure is usually just

a lot of hard work. That willingness to work hard and stick with an idea is probably the single most important requirement for becoming an entrepreneur.

The second requirement is to get some training. The educational route to becoming an entrepreneur is not as clearly mapped as it is for many other professions. Some recycling entrepreneurs are well-trained businesspeople. They've studied business in college and may even have earned an MBA (master's degree in business administration). They choose to apply their business knowledge to recycling projects.

Others are experienced in a particular field, such as manufacturing, and they add a new twist to what they've done in other jobs. Some are people who want to be their own boss and who like the idea of combining business with saving the environment. These people may learn about business by taking classes at a college or chamber of commerce or may seek help from a government-sponsored small business assistance center.

Starting a business is not the only way to base a career on environmental concerns. There are many ways to make a living while making a difference. It's up to you to start finding the best opportunities for you as a future entrepreneur.

TRY IT OUT

GARBAGE GOLDMINE

Take a look at some of the stuff you and your family throw out. Could you alter it and reuse it? How about those old boxes? Can you paint and decorate them and then use them to organize all the stuff in your room? Old egg cartons, coffee cans, and popsicle sticks make great ingredients for art projects. Save some of them in a neat place where they won't get in the way and look for ways to reuse them. For more ideas for turning trash into treasures, check out Make Stuff at http://www.makestuff.com.

CAN IT
Begin collecting aluminum cans as you find them. Start at home, then check with neighbors and other people you know. Crush them to make them more compact. Then take them to a can recycling center to earn extra money. You won't get rich doing this (unless you collect an awful lot of cans), but you'll learn something about the recycling industry and you'll do a good thing for planet Earth in the process.

WEARABLE TRASH
Don't throw that stuff away—wear it instead! Learn how to make a unique fashion statement in George Pfiffner's book *Earth-Friendly Wearables: How to Make Fabulous Clothes and Accessories from Reusable Objects* (New York: John Wiley & Sons, 1995).

RULE THE TRASH HEAP
There are lots of websites you can visit for environmentally friendly information and fun. Start with some of these.

☀ For an introduction to recycling industries, log onto the Amazing Environmental Organization WebDirectory! (http://www.webdirectory.com/Recycling).
☀ For a ton of information about recycled products, go to Global Recycling Network (http://grn.com).

Just for fun, try these sites too.

☀ Go to http://aggie-horticulture.tamu.edu/sustainable/slidesets/kidscompost/kid1.htm for a good description of how to compost your garbage.
☀ Go to http://lifelab.ucsc.edu/LifeLab/workshops.html to find ideas for lots of fun projects.

CHECK IT OUT

Association of Battery Recyclers
P.O. Box Drawer 707
Troy, Alabama 36081

Automotive Dismantlers and Recyclers Association
10400 Eaton Place
Fairfax, Virginia 22030-2208

Center for Plastics Recycling Research
Building 3529
Bush Campus Rutgers
Piscataway, New Jersey 08855-1179

Eco-Cycle
P.O. Box 19006
Boulder, Colorado 80306-9006
http://ecocycle.org

Institute for Recyclable Materials
College of Engineering
Louisiana State University
Baton Rouge, Louisiana 70803

KIDS for a Clean Environment
P.O. Box 158254
Nashville, Tennessee 37215

National Association for Plastic Container Recovery
4828 Parkway Plaza Boulevard, Suite 260
Charlotte, North Carolina 28217

Plastics Recycling Foundation, Inc.
P.O. Box 189
Kennett Square, Pennsylvania 19348

Recycler's Trade Network
950 North Rangeline Road, Suite E
Carmel, Indiana 46032

Steel Can Recycling Institute
Foster Plaza 10
680 Andersen Drive
Pittsburgh, Pennsylvania 15220

GET ACQUAINTED

Larry Sokolowski,
Recycling Entrepreneur

CAREER PATH

CHILDHOOD ASPIRATION: To be a farmer.

FIRST JOB: Working on his family's dairy farm in Wisconsin.

CURRENT JOB: Director of operations for a grease recycling company.

GREASE GUZZLER

Have you ever wondered what happens to the grease that is used to fry those delicious golden french fries you buy at fast-food restaurants? It's not just poured down the sink drain. It's picked up from special holding tanks at restaurants by special companies such as Larry Sokolowski's.

Workers drive a large, specially designed truck up to the tank. The tank is lifted into the truck, where it is heated to liquefy the grease. The grease is then poured into a separate storage compartment on the truck. The liquid grease is next taken to a processing plant that filters out all of the breading, leftover french fries, and residue that accumulate during the food preparation process. The purified grease is blended with corn and soybeans and sold as feed for chickens. The leftover breading and french fries are pressed into a cake that is high in protein and calories and is also used as chicken feed. The recycled grease is also used by chemical companies to make soap and cosmetics.

A NATURAL FIT

As he was growing up, Sokolowski did just about every one of the many jobs on his family's dairy farm. He loved being outdoors and working with the cattle. He was a member of a 4-H club and showed some of the prize-winning, registered dairy cattle they raised. He developed a respect for the natural world.

Later he worked with a municipal wastewater treatment facility. There the biosolids were processed (recycled) into a product that was sold to farmers for fertilizer. Still oriented toward the recycling industry, he next formed a partnership with a friend and began hauling liquid wastes. For the first few years it was an uncertain thing, but as they built their client base they were able to expand. They increased the number of trucks in their fleet and began to do work farther from home. After a while, they grew so big that they became a public company with shares traded on the stock exchange. When that business went public, he sold his interest for a tidy profit and got involved with the grease recycling company for which he now works.

NEVER A DULL MOMENT

Much of Sokolowski's time is now spent doing the things that most businesspeople do: marketing, working on the computer, dealing with employees and customers, and making the decisions necessary to run the business. He talks with a wide variety of people, from professors and manufacturing plant managers to private restaurant owners and truck drivers.

His employees mean a lot to him. He says they make it great to come to work each day. The company seldom has job openings since people tend to stay a long time.

The variety is another part of the job that makes it fun for Sokolowski. Every day is a little different from the one before.

PRESSURE COOKER

Competition can be intense at times. The pressure of owning a business and making decisions that work for everyone involved can make the job tough. In this business, the profit left over after all the bills are paid is sometimes very small. It is very hard for the company to sell its services as being different or better than their competitors'. Grease is grease. Just get it out of here safely.

In order to make money, the company pitches the protein value of its grease. Grease is cheaper to process than corn and soybeans are to grow. That means feeding chickens with grease-based foods is cheaper for farmers. It helps to position the product like this, but it doesn't stop Sokolowski from continually looking for new ways to use and sell this recycled material.

SOUND BUSINESS ADVICE

Sokolowski says that in order to succeed as a recycling entrepreneur, you have to have good management skills, be able to communicate well, and understand business math. The most important thing to remember is to be flexible. Solving problems requires creativity and looking for new angles in old problems.

Sokolowski urges young entrepreneurs to be willing to color outside the lines and go in a totally new direction. To do this, Sokolowski suggests young people keep up on technology and get involved with activities that develop creativity and emphasize the cutting edge. Let your imagination run wild!

Veterinarian

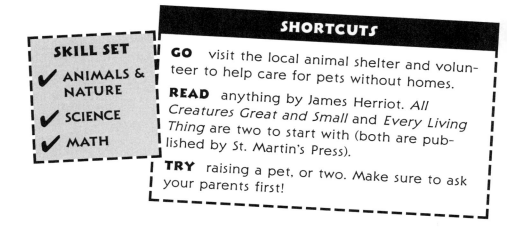

WHAT IS A VETERINARIAN?

A veterinarian loves animals and devotes his or her professional life to taking care of them. A veterinarian knows as much about animals as a medical doctor knows about people; in fact, the jobs are very similar. Animals get sick just like humans do. Animals get hurt in accidents just like humans do. A veterinarian is a doctor who treats animals.

Most veterinarians care for companion animals or pets such as dogs, cats, and birds. Many run their own private clinics and carry the same responsibilities as other business owners and employers. A typical day at a clinic might involve immunizing a dozen dogs of various breeds, neutering or spaying a cat or two, performing emergency surgery on an animal that's been hit by a car, and setting some broken bones.

Large animal vets specialize in just that—large animals. Their time might be spent at a farm, ranch, or zoo helping a lamb give birth, immunizing an entire herd of cattle, or giving nature a hand by artificially inseminating a horse. While most of their work is done during regular business hours, both types of vets must be ready to respond to middle-of-the-night emergencies.

Most of the routine tasks performed by a vet can be summed up in two categories: doing things to keep animals

healthy—regular checkups, shots, and tests—and doing things to help sick animals get better—diagnosing diseases, prescribing medication, performing surgery, and treating injuries.

While most veterinarians care for pets and farm animals in animal hospitals or clinics, other vets

- ☼ care for animals used in sporting events, such as horse races
- ☼ care for laboratory animals used in scientific studies
- ☼ care for zoo or aquarium animals
- ☼ specialize in areas such as surgery, anesthesiology, microbiology, and pathology

Another option for veterinarians is public health work. These vets work for federal agencies such as the Food and Drug Administration or the Centers for Disease Control, as

well as other state and local agencies. Some of the responsibilities of vets in public health might include

- protecting humans against diseases carried by animals
- inspecting livestock and foods
- conducting research and testing biological products such as vaccines
- evaluating new drugs to prevent or treat diseases in humans and animals

Veterinarians must complete a rigorous college program to earn their doctorate degree in veterinary medicine. This training generally takes six to eight years to complete. For those who want to work with animals but don't want to commit to that much schooling, becoming a veterinary technician is an option. This route requires only two years of college and certification by a professional organization such as the American Veterinary Medicine Association. Veterinary technicians assist vets in many ways, including caring for hospitalized patients, conducting routine laboratory tests, taking X rays, and assisting in surgical procedures. They may also find jobs with various public health organizations, research facilities, pharmaceutical manufacturers, and other types of businesses related to animal care.

Unlike the fictional Dr. Doolittle, most of the communicating vets do is with people. They must be prepared to share the joy of a new litter of pups as well as the sorrow of euthanizing a dearly loved, hopelessly sick pet with the owners. It's important work. Just ask anyone who has ever loved a pet.

TRY IT OUT

KNOW-IT-ALL NOTEBOOK

If you want to make animals the center of your career, you're going to have to start learning about them. Get a three-ring binder, some dividers, and some paper. Then stop and think before you do the next part.

How you organize your binder will depend on how deeply you want to delve into the animal kingdom. You can divide the notebook according to categories of animals: companion animals (pets), large animals (the kind found on farms and ranches), exotic animals (reptiles and birds), and zoo animals. Or you can get more specific with individual species and devote entire sections to dogs, cats, horses, etc. You decide and get it organized.

Next, you'll want to find out all you can about these animals and write down the details. Find or draw a picture to include with each summary. Make sure to include information about feeding and breeding habits, life expectancy, and common personality traits.

The library, of course, can be a great source of information, as can the Internet. Look in encyclopedias. Clip pictures from old magazines. Use a computer search engine to look for information on specific types of animals. Download photos from Internet websites.

Keep working on this project bit by bit until you've compiled as many animal facts as you can. Before you know it, you'll be a certified animal know-it-all!

TWENTY-FIRST-CENTURY VETS

Veterinary wanna-bes can find all kinds of information on the Internet. A few sites that aspiring vets won't want to miss include

- FutureScan's I Want to Be a Veterinarian at http://www.futurescan.com/vet/index.html
- NetVet at http://www.avma.org/netvet
- Virtual Veterinary Center at http://www-sci.lib.uci.edu/HSG/Vet.html
- Vetworld at http://www.vetworld.com

If you get tired of all the serious stuff, take a break at the American Veterinary Medicine Association's Kids Korner at http://www.avma.org/care4pets/avmakids.htm.

STRAIGHT FROM THE HORSE'S MOUTH

Find out what it's really like to be a vet by reading books written by veterinarians about various aspects of their profession. Here is some suggested reading for future veterinarians.

Drum, Sue, and H. E. Whitley. *Women in Veterinary Medicine: Profiles of Success.* Ames, Iowa: Iowa State University Press, 1991.

Gage, Loretta, and Nancy Gage. *If Wishes Were Horses.* New York: St. Martin's Press, 1993.

Gutkind, Lee. *An Unspoken Art: Profiles of Veterinary Life.* New York: Henry Holt, 1997.

Maze, Stephanie. *I Want to Be a Veterinarian.* New York: Harcourt Brace, 1990.

Schomp, Virginia. *If You Were a Veterinarian.* Tarrytown, N.Y.: Marshall Cavendish, 1997.

ANIMAL KEEPER FOR HIRE

Get some firsthand experience caring for animals. You need to know how well you handle the responsibility and how much you enjoy it. The experience will also help you when it comes time to apply to vet school—previous work with animals is considered a plus. A few suggestions of where you could get some experience are as follows:

- ☼ at a pet store, vet's office, farm, ranch, horse stable, or zoo doing part-time work (be prepared for some of the dirty work—it comes with the territory)
- ☼ at an animal shelter on a volunteer basis or if your parents agree, with an animal foster care program like MAXFund
- ☼ at a local 4-H group—most of these offer a variety of animal care programs

CHECK IT OUT

American Veterinary Medical Association
1931 North Meacham Road, Suite 100
Schaumburg, Illinois 60173-4360
http://www.avma.org

Association of American Veterinary Medical Colleges
1101 Vermont Avenue NW, Suite 710
Washington, D.C. 20005-3521

North American Veterinary Technician Association
P.O. Box 224
Battle Ground, Indiana 47290

GET ACQUAINTED

Christine Foster,
Veterinarian

CAREER PATH

CHILDHOOD ASPIRATION: To be a vet.

FIRST JOB: Working for a vet as a kennel attendant.

CURRENT JOB: Veterinarian in charge of Companion Paws, a mobile veterinary practice.

A PERFECT FIT

Christine Foster confesses that as a child, she sometimes liked animals more than people. She was drawn to animals and has always felt a special bond with them. Caring for one of her first pets, a brain-damaged cat, sparked Foster's interest in caring for animals at a higher level.

Foster grew up in Mexico and Brazil where her father worked for the foreign service. She says she always managed to have a couple of pets around the house even in these faraway posts. In fact, her love of cats became so well-known that people would sometimes dump stray cats over her family's fence, knowing that she'd take good care of them.

While she was in high school, Foster started working at a nearby vet's office. She began as a kennel attendant, and her main jobs were to keep the cages clean and walk the dogs. She continued working for the same vet throughout high school and college and eventually assumed the role of veterinary assistant, helping out during surgeries, prepping patients for treatment, and doing some lab work. By the time she graduated from vet school, she had earned herself a well-deserved position as associate veterinarian with the same vet who had nurtured her interest in the profession all along.

VET ON WHEELS

After 10 years working with her mentor's practice, Foster decided it was time to strike out on her own. However, after investigating the costs of starting her own practice and the needs of the pet owners in her area, she set up a practice with an interesting twist. Instead of having her patients come to her, she goes to them in a high-tech veterinary clinic on wheels. This approach especially appeals to pet owners with busy work schedules and to those, such as the elderly and disabled, who would have a hard time getting pets to a regular clinic. Of course, people with lots of pets also appreciate not having to load up a mob of animals and cart them to a clinic.

Foster's clinic consists of a 24-foot van specially equipped to handle everything from routine dental care and shots to surgery. There is even a pharmacy, X-ray machine, and electrocardiogram equipment. Almost anything a vet can do in an animal hospital, Foster can do in the driveway of the pet's own home.

ON THE RUN

Foster says that about 70 percent of any given day is devoted to routine care in which she examines pets and provides vaccines and other types of preventive care. The exciting part of the practice comes when she has to diagnose diseases. Just like doctors who work with humans, Foster does this by looking at symptoms, running tests, and putting all the pieces together to determine what's wrong. Animals get diseases such as cancer and arthritis too, and Foster especially enjoys the opportunity to help them get better.

A typical day involves making at least 10 stops, with Foster sometimes seeing several patients at each stop. A recent day involved visiting two cats with "behavior problems," giving an insulin injection to a diabetic cat whose owner was out of town, removing the sutures from a cat who had been spayed earlier in the week, and neutering a dog. Surgical procedures can take up to two or three hours while Foster puts the animal to sleep, provides the treatment, and waits for the animal to wake up and stabilize.

FOR FUTURE VETS

Foster realizes she had a truly unique experience in finding her niche in life so easily. It's not often that a person's first job leads to their dream career. She feels lucky in that regard but encourages young people with an interest in veterinary medicine to do what she did: to get a job working with animals, even if it's as a volunteer or if it involves mucking stalls. You'll learn a lot about yourself and about animals and discover if a career with animals is right for you.

She also encourages future vets to load up on science courses. She says that the biology, chemistry, and physics she took in high school helped prepare her for the rigors and excitement of vet school.

Zoologist

WHAT IS A ZOOLOGIST?

The career of zoologist does not make regular appearances on "top careers for the future" lists. That's not because it isn't a great job. The reason is that there tend to be more people who want jobs in zoos than there are jobs in zoos.

So it's a numbers game. But someone has to take care of all those animals, right? Why not you? If you are totally and completely smitten with the idea of having a career in a zoo, hang on to your dream and read on to find out more about what you might expect.

Strictly speaking, a zoologist is an expert in the biological science of animals. If you want to get technical, a zoologist is a biologist who studies the structures, characteristics, functions, ecology, and environments of animals to increase scientific knowledge and develop practical applications in wildlife management, conservation, agriculture, and medicine. In a zoo setting, zoologists apply this expertise in several different ways.

At one of the highest levels, zoologists conduct research or field studies and use their scientific findings to help zoos manage their animal collections. With a current trend toward making zoos more environmentally "natural" for animals, it wouldn't be unusual for zoologists to study the native habitat of a particular type of animal and recommend how to translate that type of environment into a zoo setting.

These zoologists might also spend a good deal of time writing research papers and educating others about their findings. In fact, they may spend as much time with books and other research tools as they do with animals.

Another way that zoologists put their animal know-how to work includes working as a zoo director, or zoo curator. Director or curator is the title given to those who oversee the operations of a specific unit of a zoo. A unit might include the mammals, the reptiles, or the birds. The zoo director or curator may be in charge of maintaining the budget, planning

nutrition programs and feeding schedules, adding new exhibits, and acquiring new animals. Some may also be responsible for developing programs to educate the public.

While zoologists may be responsible for the entire operation of a zoo program, a zookeeper is responsible for the day-to-day care and feeding of one or more specific animal "houses" in the zoo. Whether it's giraffes, lions, or penguins, the zookeeper is almost like a parent to the animals in their care. They do everything necessary to make sure that the animals are well fed, clean, and healthy—even if it means exercising an elephant or brushing a monkey's teeth.

Other professions well represented in zoos include animal trainers, zoo veterinarians, aquarists (who tend to sea creatures and fish), and horticulturists (who tend to plant life and zoo gardens). Opportunities for those who like animals and nature are varied at the typical zoo.

There are two ways to prepare yourself for one of the coveted positions in a zoo or aquarium: education and experience. Regarding education, plan on earning a college degree with a major in zoology, animal science, marine biology, conservation biology, wildlife management, or animal behavior. Those aspiring to curatorial, research, and conservation positions will need to get an advanced degree at some point in their career.

The other, unavoidable, way to prepare yourself for a zoo career is experience. There is a big (make that *huge*) difference between reading about caring for animals and actually caring for animals. There is just no substitute for on-the-job training. Volunteer positions and internships are good ways to get started. Working as an assistant to a zookeeper or curator is often the first step for someone pursuing a career in zoos.

If zoos are your thing but you have concerns about the odds for a career in zoology, don't overlook the obvious. Animal care isn't the only way to land a fun job at a zoo. Any job that you can do in another kind of business you can also do at a zoo. Accounting, administration, marketing, public relations, personnel, food service, management—all the business bases are covered to provide plenty of approaches to finding your place at the zoo.

TRY IT OUT

SPEND THE DAY AT THE ZOO

Thanks to the wonders of modern technology, it doesn't matter if you live in a great big city or a tiny town. Log on to the Internet and you can enjoy the wonders of zoos at far-flung corners of the world.

Start your zoo adventure at the National Zoo (http://www.si.edu/organiza/museums/zoo/nzphome.htm). Next, crisscross the country for a quick stop at the world famous San Diego Zoo (http://www.sandiegozoo.org). Following this, take a scenic tour up the coast and visit the Sacramento Zoo (http://www.saczoo.com). Then travel back east to New York and stop by the Bronx Zoo (http://www.bronxzoo.com). Then cyber-travel to the nation's oldest zoo, Chicago's Lincoln Park Zoo (http://www.lpzoo.com). Getting jetlag? Try a tour of the Virtual Zoo (http://www.thezoo.org/vz).

If you have a favorite zoo not listed here, use an Internet search engine such as Yahoo! (http://www.yahoo.com) or HotBot (http://www.hotbot.com) to see if it has an Internet website.

A DAY IN THE LIFE OF AN ELEPHANT

For an in-the-know look at what it's like to be a zookeeper in charge of the elephants at the Indianapolis Zoo, check out the "day in the life of an elephant" link via the American Association of Zoo Keepers at http://www.aazk.org. First, click on the Zookeeping-as-a-career icon, then click on the Day with the Elephants link.

Speaking of elephant zookeepers, why not give that job a try yourself? First you must learn all you can about your gigantic friends. Start your search at a website devoted exclusively to pachydermia (that's scientific lingo for elephant, rhino, and related animal stuff). It's found at http://home.onestop.net/wrath/elephant.html and contains links to all kinds of interesting elephant-related websites.

For a quick look at some important facts about an elephant-friendly diet, habitat, and behavior tips, check out http://www.wildlifeafrica.co.za/elephantbehavior.html.

Print out interesting information and keep track of the facts you discover. Once you've gathered all the data, make a chart showing what you would do if you were zookeeper of the elephants for a day. What would you feed them? What kind of environment would you prepare for them? How would you make sure they had proper conditions for exercise and socializing? Think of all it would take to keep the herd happy for the day and jot it down on your chart.

WILD AND CRAZY FUN

Remember, a zoologist is an animal expert. Since experts are not made overnight, you should start learning all you can about the animal kingdom now. While you're at it, have some fun too at sites such as

- ☿ Amazing Animal Facts at http://zebu.cvm.msu.edu/~dawsonbr/amaze.htm
- ☿ Trivia Animal at http://parcsafari.qc.ca/english/triviae.htm
- ☿ Animal Guessing Game at http://www.bushnet.qld.edu.au/animal
- ☿ Zooary at http://www.bonus.com/bonus/card/zooary.html

You might want to use 3-by-5-inch index cards to keep track of all that you learn. Use the cards to make up your animal games.

THE WELL-READ ZOOLOGIST

There's nothing like a good book to take you places you can only dream about right now. Fuel your dreams of becoming a zoologist with books such as these.

Cohen, Judith L. *You Can Be a Woman Zoologist.* Culver City, Calif.: Cascade Pass, 1994.

Deedrick, Tami. *Zoo Keepers.* Minneapolis, Minn.: Capstone Press, 1998.

Knight, Bertram T. *Working at a Zoo.* Danbury, Conn.: Children's Press, 1999.

Maynard, Thane. *Endangered Animal Babies: Saving Species One Birth at a Time.* Danbury, Conn.: Franklin Watts, 1993.

Thompson, Kim M. *I'd Like to Be a Zoologist: Learning About Mammals, Reptiles, and Amphibians.* Akron, Ohio: Twin Sisters Productions, 1997.

WHAT A ZOO!

How in the world is a kid like you supposed to try out being a zoologist? Like they're really going to put you in the middle of a lion's cage to see what you think. Like you'd really want to go anywhere near a lion's cage to find out!

Fortunately, there are some less risky ways to find out if zoos are the place for you. Try some of the projects described in the following books to get a feel for what it's like to be a zoologist.

Dashefsky, H. Steven. *Zoology: 49 Science Fair Projects.* New York: McGraw-Hill, 1994.

Doris, Ellen. *Invertebrate Zoology.* New York: Thames & Hudson, 1993.

Dystra, Mary. *The Amateur Zoologist: Explorations and Investigations.* Danbury, Conn.: Franklin Watts, 1994.

Gardner, Robert, and David Webster. *Science Project Ideas About Animal Behavior.* Springfield, N.J.: Enslow Publishers, 1997.

VanCleave, Janice. *Janice VanCleave's Animals: Spectacular Science Projects.* New York: John Wiley & Sons, 1992.

CHECK IT OUT

American Association of Zoo Keepers
Topeka Zoological Park
635 S.W. Gage Boulevard
Topeka, Kansas 66606-2066
http://www.aazk.org/aazk

American Association of Zoo Veterinarians
6 North Pennell Road
Media, Pennsylvania 19063
http://www.worldzoo.org/aazv

American Zoo and Aquarium Association
Olgebay Park
Wheeling, West Virginia 26003
http://www.aza.org

Association of Zoo and Aquarium Docents
Columbus Zoological Gardens
P.O. Box 400
Powell, Ohio 43065-0400
http://www.colszoo.org/volunteer.html

Society for Integrative and Comparative Biology
401 North Michigan Avenue
Chicago, Illinois 60611
http://www.sicb.org

GET ACQUAINTED

Kathy Marmack,
Zookeeper

CAREER PATH

CHILDHOOD ASPIRATION: To work with animals.

FIRST JOB: Assistant to a dog obedience instructor when she was 12.

CURRENT JOB: Animal trainer supervisor at the San Diego Zoo.

THE RIGHT PLACE AT THE RIGHT TIME

Kathy Marmack has always known that she had a future with animals. It seems like fate has agreed with her along the way, because she seems to always be in the right place at the right time for keeping her animal career on track.

It all started when she was 12 years old. She started hanging around the local parks and recreation center during the dog obedience classes. She didn't have a dog that needed training; she was just intrigued with how the instructor could come into a room full of misbehaving dogs and achieve order with a few seemingly simple commands.

The instructor, a retired humane service officer, took notice and asked Marmack if she'd like to learn how to do it. Would she? You bet! Before you could say "sit," Marmack had learned the basics and was hired to help some of the problem students in the next class.

To this day, Marmack is grateful for this experience. Not only did she learn how to train dogs, but as a child responsible for helping adults learn how to work with their dogs, Marmack learned valuable people skills that have served her well throughout her career.

THANK THOSE LUCKY STARS!

Marmack was hooked on working with animals but not sure what to do after she graduated from high school. As good luck would have it, Marmack took her puppy to the vet for shots one day, the vet just happened to be looking for an assistant, and Marmack walked out with a job. Working at the vet's office she learned more about handling animals and earning their trust.

Looking toward the future, Marmack decided she'd like to prepare herself to become a state humane officer (more commonly known as a dog catcher). At the time, California law required humane officers to have experience in law enforcement, so Marmack spent her after work hours training as a reserve sheriff.

Once again, Marmack's uncanny ability to be in the right place at the right time came into play. At a sheriff's meeting someone casually mentioned that the San Diego Wild Animal Park was looking for help with some of their animal shows. Marmack jumped on the news, applied for the job (along with 28 other hopeful applicants), and ended up with the opportunity of a lifetime. It turns out one of the San Diego Zoo's premier zoologists needed an animal handler. Marmack's early experience with both animals and people made her a shoo-in for the position. She joined Joan Embery, the zoo's goodwill ambassador; Carol, the very intelligent elephant; Rufus, the timber wolf; Cody, the cougar; Frisky, the guanaco; and Anastasia, the red-tailed hawk, for an incredible start to an exciting career at the zoo.

YOU KNOW YOU'RE RIGHT FOR THE JOB WHEN . . .

Now, several years later, Marmack is in charge of the zoo's educational programs at two sites. There are 27 animals of all kinds at one site and 18 at another. Marmack is responsible for running two to four shows each day as well as everything else it takes to keep all those animals happy and healthy. Feeding, cleaning, exercising, training—you name it and chances are pretty good that Marmack does it.

Marmack admits that it sounds weird, but one of her favorite times of the day is when she gets the chance to clean the animals' compartments. It's not that she particularly enjoys scooping poop. It's just that this quiet time offers her the best chance to bond with each animal and make sure they are doing well. It's an important part of the trust process between the animals and their keeper.

DON'T TRY THIS AT HOME

Marmack's career has been unusual when it comes to her own training. Marmack has no formal training in zoology. Instead, she learned from two mentors who gave her the chance to train on the job. The first was the dog obedience instructor and the second was Embery. Marmack says she is forever indebted to these incredible role models for showing her the way.

As far as advising future zoologists, Marmack is the first one to encourage them to get all the education they can. Today it's almost impossible to get the kind of lucky breaks Marmack has enjoyed. A solid education in biology or zoology is key.

But experience is really important too. Marmack says to start now in getting involved with animals. Raise a puppy for a guide dog program, volunteer at a raptor rehabilitation program, take your dog to obedience classes, join a 4-H club—anything that gets you in touch with animals. It's the best way to find out if a career with animals is right for you.

MAKE A NATURAL DETOUR!

In case you haven't noticed, you are constanty surrounded by animals and nature. Whether it's as simple as a spider crawling across the windowsill or as spectacular as a raging thunderstorm, there's simply no escape—which is more than OK for people who are really and truly intrigued with nature's wonders.

If you are one of these people, you owe it to yourself to fully explore all the nature-related options you can imagine. You've just read about several exciting careers. Read on for more ideas to consider.

A WORLD OF CAREERS WITH GROWTH POTENTIAL

OPPORTUNITIES IN THE GREAT OUTDOORS

If you'd just as soon have your "office" outside under a tree, you'll want to take note of some of these careers that offer plenty of fresh air and sunshine.

agronomist
agriculturist
aquaculturist
cartographer
civil engineer
conservationist
ecologist
forester
gardener
geographer

land planner
landscape architect
paleontologist
plant explorer
plant physiologist
soil scientist
taxonomist
tree surgeon
water quality engineer

THE NATURE OF SCIENCE

Did you know that most of the basic biological processes are the same in both plants and animals? Here are some ways to earn a living using all you know about biology and the earth sciences.

bacteriologist
biochemist
biology teacher
biophysicist
biotechnologist
chemotaxonomist

fish biologist
genetic engineer
molecular biologist
plant pathologist
research biologist
wildlife biologist

BIRDS, BEES, AND FOUR-LEGGED FRIENDS

Animal lovers beware! There are plenty of ways to get paid for caring for your favorite creatures.

animal breeder
animal protection officer
animal therapist
aquarist
beekeeper
dog trainer

fishery scientist
horse trainer
jockey
ornithologist
pet-sitter

OUT TO SEA

Dive in and explore some of these water-related career ideas.

aquatic biologist
bridge builder
deep-sea diver
ferry boat operator
fisherman
fishery manager
harbor pilot

longshoreman
marina manager
marine engineer
naval architect
naval engineer
oceanographer

FOR THE ARTISTICALLY INCLINED

Combining artistic ability and a love of animals and nature opens some interesting career possibilities. Think of creative ways to mix the two in careers such as the ones listed below.

artist
designer
editor
illustrator

photographer
publisher
writer

INFORMATION IS POWER

Mind-boggling, isn't it? There are so many great choices, so many jobs you've never heard of before. How will you ever narrow it down to the perfect spot for you?

First, pinpoint the ideas that sound the most interesting to you. Then, find out all you can about them. As you may have noticed, a similar pattern of information was used for each of the career entries featured in this book. Each entry included

☼ a general description or definition of the career
☼ some hands-on projects that give readers a chance to actually experience a job
☼ a list of organizations to contact for more information
☼ an interview with a professional

You can use information like this to help you determine the best career path to pursue. Since there isn't room in one book to profile all these animal- and nature-related career choices, here's your chance to do it yourself. Conduct a full investigation into a career that interests you.

Please Note: **If this book does not belong to you, use a separate sheet of paper to record your responses to the following questions.**

MAKE A NATURAL DETOUR!

CAREER TITLE _____

WHAT IS A _____?
Use career encyclopedias and other
resources to write a description of this
career.

SKILL SET
✔ _____
✔ _____
✔ _____

TRY IT OUT
Write project ideas here. Ask your parents and your teacher
to come up with a plan.

CHECK IT OUT
List professional organizations where you can learn more
about this profession.

GET ACQUAINTED
Interview a professional in the field and summarize your findings.

DON'T STOP NOW!

GO FOR IT!

It's been a fast-paced trip so far. Take a break, regroup, and look at all the progress you've made.

1st Stop: Self-Discovery
You discovered some personal interests and natural abilities that you can start building a career around.

2nd Stop: Exploration
You've explored an exciting array of career opportunities involving animals and nature. You're now aware that your career can involve either a specialized area with many educational requirements or that it can involve a practical application of skills with a minimum of training and experience.

At this point, you've found a couple of (or few) careers that really intrigue you. Now it's time to put it all together and do all you can to make an informed, intelligent choice. It's time to move on.

3rd Stop: Experimentation
By the time you finish this section, you'll have reached one of three points in the career planning process.

1. **Green light!** You found it. No need to look any further. This is *the* career for you. (This may happen to a lucky few. Don't worry if it hasn't happened yet for you. This whole process is about exploring options, experimenting with ideas, and, eventually, making the best choice for you.)
2. **Yellow light!** Close, but not quite. You seem to be on the right path but you haven't nailed things down for sure. (This is where many people your age end up, and it's a good place to be. You've learned what it takes to really check things out. Hang in there. Your time will come.)
3. **Red light!** Whoa! No doubt about it, this career just isn't for you. (Congratulations! Aren't you glad you found out now and not after you'd spent four years in college preparing for this career? Your next stop: Make a U-turn and start this process over with another career.)

Here's a sneak peek at what you'll be doing in the next section.

☀ First, you'll pick a favorite career idea (or two or three).
☀ Second, you'll snoop around the library to find answers to the 10 things you've just got to know about your future career.
☀ Third, you'll pick up the phone and talk to someone whose career you admire to find out what it's really like.
☀ Fourth, you'll link up with a whole world of great information about your career idea on the Internet (it's easier than you think).
☀ Fifth, you'll go on the job to shadow a professional for a day.

Hang on to your hats and get ready to make tracks!

#1 NARROW DOWN YOUR CHOICES

You've been introduced to quite a few animal- and nature-related career ideas. You may also have some ideas of your own to add. Which ones appeal to you the most?

Write your top three choices in the spaces below. (Sorry if this is starting to sound like a broken record, but . . . **if this book does not belong to you, write your responses on a separate sheet of paper.**)

1. _____
2. _____
3. _____

WRITE YOUR RESPONSES ON A SEPARATE PIECE OF PAPER

#2 SNOOP AT THE LIBRARY

Take your list of favorite career ideas, a notebook, and a helpful adult with you to the library. When you get there, go to the reference section and ask the librarian to help you find

books about careers. Most libraries will have at least one set of career encyclopedias. Some of the larger libraries may also have career information on CD-ROM.

Gather all the information you can and use it to answer the following questions in your notebook about each of the careers on your list. Make sure to ask for help if you get stuck.

TOP 10 THINGS YOU NEED TO KNOW ABOUT YOUR CAREER

1. What kinds of skills does this job require?
2. What kind of training is required? (Compare the options for a high school degree, trade school degree, two-year degree, four-year degree, and advanced degree.)
3. What types of classes do I need to take in high school in order to be accepted into a training program?
4. What are the names of three schools or colleges where I can get the training I need?
5. Are there any apprenticeship or internship opportunities available? If so, where? If not, could I create my own opportunity? How?
6. How much money can I expect to earn as a beginner? How much with more experience?
7. What kinds of places hire people to do this kind of work?
8. What is a typical work environment like? For example, would I work in a busy office, outdoors, or in a laboratory?
9. What are some books and magazines I could read to learn more about this career? Make a list and look for them at your library.
10. Where can I write for more information? Make a list of professional associations.

#3 CHAT ON THE PHONE

Talking to a seasoned professional—someone who experiences the job day in and day out—can be a great way to get the inside story on what a career is all about. Fortunately for you, the experts in any career field can be as close as the nearest telephone.

Sure it can be a bit scary calling up an adult whom you don't know. But, two things are in your favor:

1. They can't see you. The worst thing they can do is hang up on you, so just relax and enjoy the conversation.
2. They'll probably be happy to talk to you about their job. In fact, most people will be flattered that you've called. If you happen to contact someone who seems reluctant to talk, thank them for their time and try someone else.

Here are a few pointers to help make your telephone interview a success.

- ☀ Mind your manners and speak clearly.
- ☀ Be respectful of their time and position.
- ☀ Be prepared with good questions and take notes as you talk.

One more commonsense reminder: Be careful about giving out your address and DO NOT arrange to meet anyone you don't know without your parents' supervision.

TRACKING DOWN CAREER EXPERTS

You might be wondering by now how to find someone to interview. Have no fear! It's easy, if you're persistent. All you have to do is ask. Ask the right people and you'll have a great lead in no time.

A few of the people to ask and sources to turn to are

Your parents. They may know someone (or know someone who knows someone) who has just the kind of job you're looking for.

Your friends and neighbors. You might be surprised to find out how many interesting jobs these people have when you start asking them what they (or their parents) do for a living.

Librarians. Since you've already figured out what kinds of companies employ people in your field of interest, the next step is to ask for information about local employers. Although it's a bit cumbersome to use, a big volume called *Contacts Influential* can provide this kind of information.

Professional associations. Call or write to the professional associations you discovered in Activity #1 a few pages back and ask for recommendations.

Chambers of commerce. The local chamber of commerce probably has a directory of employers, their specialties, and their phone numbers. Call the chamber, explain what you are looking for, and give the person a chance to help the future workforce.

Newspaper and magazine articles. Find an article about the subject you are interested in. Chances are pretty good that it will mention the name of at least one expert in the field. The article probably won't include the person's phone number (that would be too easy), so you'll have to look for clues. Common clues include the name of the company that the expert works for, the town that he or she lives in, and if the person is an author, the name of his or her publisher. Make a few phone calls and track the person down (if long distance calls are involved, make sure to get your parents' permission first).

INQUIRING KIDS WANT TO KNOW

Before you make the call, make a list of questions to ask. You'll cover more ground if you focus on using the five w's (and the h) that you've probably heard about in your creative writing classes: Who? What? Where? When? How? and Why? For example,

1. Who do you work for?
2. What is a typical work day like for you?
3. Where can I get some on-the-job experience?
4. When did you become a _____?
   (profession)
5. How much can you earn in this profession? (But, remember it's not polite to ask someone how much *he* or *she* earns.)
6. Why did you choose this profession?

One last suggestion: Add a professional (and very classy) touch to the interview process by following up with a thank-you note to the person who took time out of a busy schedule to talk with you.

#4 SURF THE NET

With the Internet, the new information super-highway, charging full steam ahead, you literally have a world of information at your fingertips. The Internet has something for everyone, and it's getting easier to access all the time. An increasing number of libraries and schools are

offering access to the Internet on their computers. In addition, companies such as America Online and CompuServe have made it possible for anyone with a home computer to surf the World Wide Web.

A typical career search will land everything from the latest news on developments in the field and course notes from universities to museum exhibits, interactive games, educational activities, and more. You just can't beat the timeliness or the variety of information available on the Net.

One of the easiest ways to track down this information is to use an Internet search engine, such as Yahoo! Simply type in the topic you are looking for, and in a matter of seconds, you'll have a list of options from around the world. It's fun to browse—you never know what you'll come up with.

To narrow down your search a bit, look for specific websites, forums, or chatrooms that are related to your topic in the following publications:

Gentry, Lorna, Mark Bibler, and Kelli Brooks. *New Rider's Official Internet and World Wide Web Yellow Pages.* Indianapolis, Ind.: New Rider's Publishing, 1998.

Hahn, Harley. *Harley Hahn's Internet and Web Yellow Pages.* Berkeley, Calif.: Osborne McGraw Hill, 1998.

Maxwell, Christine. *Internet Yellow Pages.* Indianapolis, Ind.: New Rider's Publishing, 1997.

Polly, Jean Armour. *The Internet Kids and Family Yellow Pages.* Berkeley, Calif.: Osborne McGraw Hill, 1998.

To go on-line at home you may want to compare two of the more popular on-line services: America Online and CompuServe. Please note that there is a monthly subscription fee for using these services. There can also be extra fees attached to specific forums and services, so *make sure you have your parents' OK before you sign up.* For information

about America Online call 800-827-6364. For information about CompuServe call 800-848-8990. Both services frequently offer free start-up deals, so shop around.

There are also many other services, depending on where you live. Check your local phone book or ads in local computer magazines for other service options.

Before you link up, keep in mind that many of these sites are geared toward professionals who are already working in a particular field. Some of the sites can get pretty technical. Just use the experience as a chance to nose around the field, hang out with the people who are tops in the field, and think about whether or not you'd like to be involved in a profession like that.

Specific sites to look for are the following:

Professional associations. Find out about what's happening in the field, conferences, journals, and other helpful tidbits.

Schools that specialize in this area. Many include research tools, introductory courses, and all kinds of interesting information.

Government agencies. Quite a few are going high-tech with lots of helpful resources.

Websites hosted by experts in the field (this seems to be a popular hobby among many professionals). These websites are often as entertaining as they are informative.

If you're not sure where to go, just start clicking around. Sites often link to other sites. You may want to jot down notes about favorite sites. Sometimes you can even print out information that isn't copyright-protected; try the print option and see what happens.

Be prepared: Surfing the Internet can be an addicting habit! There is so much great information. It's a fun way to focus on your future.

#5 SHADOW A PROFESSIONAL

Linking up with someone who is gainfully employed in a profession that you want to explore is a great way to find out what a career is like. Following someone around while the person is at work is called "shadowing." Try it!

This process involves three steps.

1. Find someone to shadow. Some suggestions include
   - ☿ the person you interviewed (if you enjoyed talking with him or her and feel comfortable about asking the person to show you around the workplace)
   - ☿ friends and neighbors (you may even be shocked to discover that your parents have interesting jobs)
   - ☿ workers at the chamber of commerce may know of mentoring programs available in your area (it's a popular concept, so most larger areas should have something going on)
   - ☿ someone at your local School-to-Work office, the local Boy Scouts Explorer program director (this is available to girls too!), or your school guidance counselor
2. Make a date. Call and make an appointment. Find out when is the best time for arrival and departure. Make arrangements with a parent or other respected adult to go with you and get there on time.
3. Keep your ears and eyes open. This is one time when it is OK to be nosy. Ask

questions. Notice everything that is happening around you. Ask your host to let you try some of the tasks he or she is doing.

The basic idea of the shadowing experience is to put yourself in the other person's shoes and see how they fit. Imagine yourself having a job like this 10 or 15 years down the road. It's a great way to find out if you are suited for a particular line of work.

BE CAREFUL OUT THERE!

Two cautions must accompany this recommendation. First, remember the "stranger danger" rules of your childhood. NEVER meet with anyone you don't know without your parents' permission and ALWAYS meet in a supervised situation—at the office or with your parents.

Second, be careful not to overdo it. These people are busy earning a living, so respect their time by limiting your contact and coming prepared with valid questions and background information.

PLAN B

If shadowing opportunities are limited where you live, try one of these approaches for learning the ropes from a professional.

Pen pals. Find a mentor who is willing to share information, send interesting materials, or answer specific questions that come up during your search.

Cyber pals. Go on-line in a forum or chatroom related to your profession. You'll be able to chat with professionals from all over the world.

If you want to get some more on-the-job experience, try one of these approaches.

Volunteer to do the dirty work. Volunteer to work for someone who has a job that interests you for a specified period of time. Do anything—filing, errands, emptying trash cans—that puts you in contact with professionals. Notice every tiny detail about the profession. Listen to the lingo they use in the profession. Watch how they perform their jobs on a day-to-day basis.

Be an apprentice. This centuries-old job training method is making a comeback. Find out if you can set up an official on-the-job training program to gain valuable experience. Ask professional associations about apprenticeship opportunities. Once again, a School-to-Work program can be a great asset. In many areas, they've established some very interesting career training opportunities.

Hire yourself for the job. Maybe you are simply too young to do much in the way of on-the-job training right now. That's OK. Start learning all you can now and you'll be ready to really wow them when the time is right. Make sure you do all the Try It Out activities included for the career(s) you are most interested in. Use those activities as a starting point for creating other projects that will give you a feel for what the job is like.

WHAT'S NEXT?

Have you carefully worked your way through all of the suggested activities? You haven't tried to sneak past anything, have you? This isn't a place for shortcuts. If you've done the activities, you're ready to decide where you stand with each career idea. So what is it? Green light? See page 166. Yellow light? See page 165. Red light? See page 164. Find the spot that best describes your response to what you've discovered about this career idea and plan your next move.

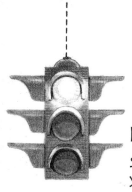

RED LIGHT

So you've decided this career is definitely not for you—hang in there! The process of elimination is an important one. You've learned some valuable career planning skills; use them to explore other ideas. In the meantime, use the following road map to chart a plan to get beyond this "spinning your wheels" point in the process.

Take a variety of classes at school to expose yourself to new ideas and expand the options. Make a list of courses you want to try.

- ☀ _WRITE YOUR RESPONSES ON_
- ☀ _A SEPARATE PIECE OF PAPER_
- ☀
- ☀

Get involved in clubs and other after-school activities (like 4-H or Boy Scout Explorers) to further develop your interests. Write down some that interest you.

- ☀ _WRITE YOUR RESPONSES ON_
- ☀ _A SEPARATE PIECE OF PAPER_
- ☀
- ☀

Read all you can find about interesting people and their work. Make a list of people you'd like to learn more about.

- ☀ _WRITE YOUR RESPONSES ON_
- ☀ _A SEPARATE PIECE OF PAPER_
- ☀
- ☀

Keep at it. Time is on your side. Finding the perfect work for you is worth a little effort. Once you've crossed this hurdle, move on to the next pages and continue mapping out a great future.

YELLOW LIGHT

Proceed with caution. While the idea continues to intrigue you, you may wonder if it's the best choice for you. Your concerns are legitimate (listen to that nagging little voice inside!).

Maybe it's the training requirements that intimidate you. Maybe you have concerns about finding a good job once you complete the training. Maybe you wonder if you have what it takes to do the job.

At this point, it's good to remember that there is often more than one way to get somewhere. Check out all the choices and choose the route that's best for you. Use the following road map to move on down the road in your career planning adventure.

Make two lists. On the first, list the things you like most about the career you are currently investigating. On the second, list the things that are most important to you in a future career. Look for similarities on both lists and focus on careers that emphasize these similar key points.

Current Career	Future Career
☼ _____	☼ _____
☼ _____	☼ _____

What are some career ideas that are similar to the one you have in mind? Find out all you can about them. Go back through the exploration process explained on pages 153 to 162 and repeat some of the exercises that were most valuable.

☼ _____

☼ _____

☼ _____

☼ _____

WRITE YOUR RESPONSES ON
A SEPARATE PIECE OF PAPER

Visit your school counselor and ask him or her which career assessment tools are available through your school. Use these to find out more about your strengths and interests. List the date, time, and place for any assessment tests you plan to take.

☼ _WRITE YOUR RESPONSES ON_
☼ _A SEPARATE PIECE OF PAPER_
☼
☼

What other adults do you know and respect to whom you can talk about your future? They may have ideas that you've never thought of.

☼ _WRITE YOUR RESPONSES ON_
☼ _A SEPARATE PIECE OF PAPER_
☼
☼

What kinds of part-time jobs, volunteer work, or after-school experiences can you look into that will give you a chance to build your skills and test your abilities? Think about how you can tap into these opportunities.

☼ _WRITE YOUR RESPONSES ON_
☼ _A SEPARATE PIECE OF PAPER_
☼
☼

GREEN LIGHT

Yahoo! You are totally turned on to this career idea and ready to do whatever it takes to make it your life's work. Go for it!

Find out what kinds of classes you need to take now to prepare for this career. List them here.

☼ _WRITE YOUR RESPONSES ON_
☼ _A SEPARATE PIECE OF PAPER_
☼
☼

What are some on-the-job training possibilities for you to pursue? List the company name, a person to contact, and the phone number.

WRITE YOUR RESPONSES ON A SEPARATE PIECE OF PAPER

Find out if there are any internship or apprenticeship opportunities available in this career field. List contacts and phone numbers.

WRITE YOUR RESPONSES ON A SEPARATE PIECE OF PAPER

What kind of education will you need after you graduate from high school? Describe the options.

WRITE YOUR RESPONSES ON A SEPARATE PIECE OF PAPER

No matter what the educational requirements are, the better your grades are during junior and senior high school, the better your chances for the future.

Take a minute to think about some areas that need improvement in your schoolwork. Write your goals for giving it all you've got here.

WRITE YOUR RESPONSES ON A SEPARATE PIECE OF PAPER

Where can you get the training you'll need? Make a list of colleges, technical schools, or vocational programs. Include addresses so that you can write to request a catalog.

☼ _____

☼ _____

☼ _____

☼ _____

WRITE YOUR RESPONSES ON A SEPARATE PIECE OF PAPER

HOORAY! YOU DID IT!

This has been quite a trip. If someone tries to tell you that this process is easy, don't believe it. Figuring out what you want to do with the rest of your life is heavy stuff, and it should be. If you don't put some thought (and some sweat and hard work) into the process, you'll get stuck with whatever comes your way.

You may not have things planned to a T. Actually, it's probably better if you don't. You'll change some of your ideas as you grow and experience new things. And, you may find an interesting detour or two along the way. That's OK.

The most important thing about beginning this process now is that you've started to dream. You've discovered that you have some unique talents and abilities to share. You've become aware of some of the ways you can use them to make a living—and, perhaps, make a difference in the world.

Whatever you do, don't lose sight of the hopes and dreams you've discovered. You've got your entire future ahead of you. Use it wisely.

SOME FUTURE DESTINATIONS

Wow! You've really made tracks during this whole process. Now that you've gotten this far, you'll want to keep moving forward to a great future. This section will point you toward some useful resources to help you make a conscientious career choice (that's just the opposite of falling into any old job on a fluke).

IT'S NOT JUST FOR NERDS

The school counselor's office is not just a place where teachers send troublemakers. One of its main purposes is to help students like you make the most of your educational opportunities. Most schools will have a number of useful resources, including career assessment tools (ask about the Self-Directed Search Career Explorer or the COPS Interest Inventory—these are especially useful assessments for people your age). There may also be a stash of books, videos, and other helpful materials.

Make sure no one's looking and sneak into your school counseling office to get some expert advice!

AWESOME INTERNET CAREER RESOURCES

Your parents will be green with envy when they see all the career planning resources you have at your fingertips. Get ready to hear them whine, "But they didn't have all this stuff when I was a kid." Make the most of these cyberspace opportunities.

- ☼ You'll find links to all kinds of fun information in the Awesome Library at http://www.neat_schoolhouse. org/Library/reference_and_Periodicals/Job_Search_Center/ Career_Exploration_for_Teens.html.
- ☼ Future Scan includes in-depth profiles on a wide variety of career choices and expert advice from their "Guidance Gurus." Check it out at http://www.futurescan.com.
- ☼ Two sites—Kaplan (http://www.kaplan.com) and Princeton Review (http://www.review.com)—include information about specific careers as well as all kinds of information about the education you'll need to prepare for your career of choice.
- ☼ JobStar California Career Guides is another site to explore specific career choices. Look for it at http:// www.jobsmart.org/tools/career/spec-car.htm.

IT'S NOT JUST FOR BOYS

Boys and girls alike are encouraged to contact their local version of the Boy Scouts Explorer program. It offers exciting on-the-job training experiences in a variety of professional fields. Look in the white pages of your community phone book for the local Boy Scouts of America program.

MORE CAREER BOOKS ESPECIALLY FOR ANIMAL AND NATURE LOVERS

Whether it's the great outdoors or all creatures great and small that ignite your interest, here are some books that provide additional information about career opportunities.

Basta, Nicholas. *The Environmental Career Guide*. New York: John Wiley & Sons, 1991.

———. *Environmental Jobs for Scientists and Engineers*. New York: John Wiley & Sons, 1992.

Camenson, Blythe. *Opportunities in Landscape Architecture, Botanical Gardens, and Arboreta*. Lincolnwood, Ill.: VGM Career Horizons, 1998.

———. *Opportunities in Zoo Careers*. Lincolnwood, Ill.: VGM Career Horizons, 1997.

The Complete Guide to Environmental Careers. Washington, D.C.: CEIP Fund, 1989.

Fasulo, Michael, and Paul Walker. *Careers in the Environment*. Lincolnwood, Ill.: VGM Career Horizons, 1995.

Gartner, Robert. *Careers Inside the World of Environmental Science*. New York: Rosen Publishing, 1995.

Grant, Lesley. *Great Careers for People Concerned About the Environment*. Detroit: UXL, 1993.

Hurwitz, Jane. *Choosing a Career in Animal Care*. New York: Rosen Publishing, 1997.

Kinney, Jane, and Michael Fasulo. *Careers for Environmental Types and Others Who Respect the Earth*. Lincolnwood, Ill.: VGM Career Horizons, 1994.

Lee, Barbara. *Working with Animals*. Minneapolis, Minn.: Lerner Publications, 1996.

Lee, Mary Price. *Opportunities in Animal and Pet Care Careers.* Lincolnwood, Ill.: VGM Career Horizons, 1994.

Miller, Louise. *Careers for Animal Lovers and Other Zoological Types.* Lincolnwood, Ill.: VGM Career Horizons, 1991.

————. *Careers for Nature Lovers and Other Outdoor Types.* Lincolnwood, Ill.: VGM Career Horizons, 1992.

Pasternak, Ceel, and Linda Thornburg. *Cool Careers for Girls with Animals.* Manassas Park, Va.: Impact Publications, 1999.

Quintana, Debra. *100 Jobs in the Environment.* New York: Macmillan, 1996.

Warner, David J. *Environmental Careers: A Practical Guide for the 90s.* Chelsea, Mich.: Lewis Publishers, 1992.

HEAVY-DUTY RESOURCES

Career encyclopedias provide general information about a lot of professions and can be a great place to start a career search. Those listed here are easy to use and provide useful information about nearly a zillion different jobs. Look for them in the reference section of your local library.

Cosgrove, Holli, ed. *Career Discovery Encyclopedia: 1997 Edition.* Chicago: J. G. Ferguson Publishing, 1997.

Encyclopedia of Career Choices for the 1990's. New York: Perigee Books/Putnam Publishing, 1992.

Maze, Marilyn, and Donald Mayall. *The Enhanced Guide for Occupational Exploration: Descriptions for the 2,800 Most Important Jobs.* Indianapolis: JIST, 1995.

VGM's Careers Encyclopedia. Lincolnwood, Ill.: VGM Career Books, 1997.

FINDING PLACES TO WORK

Use resources like these to find leads on local businesses, mentors, job shadowing opportunities, and internships. Later, use these same resources to find a great job!

LeCompte, Michelle. *Job Hunter's Sourcebook: Where to Find Employment Leads and Other Job Search Resources.* Detroit: Gale Research, 1996.

Morgan, Bradley J., ed. *Environmental Career Directory.* Detroit: Visible Ink Press, 1993.

Also consult the Job Bank series (Holbrook, Mass.: Adams Media Group). Adams publishes separate guides for Atlanta, Seattle, and many major points in between. Ask your local librarian if the library has a guide for the biggest city near you.

FINDING PLACES TO PRACTICE JOB SKILLS

An apprenticeship is an official opportunity to learn a specific profession by working side by side with a skilled professional. As a training method, it's as old as the hills, and it's making a comeback in a big way because people are realizing that doing a job is simply the best way to learn a job.

An internship is an official opportunity to gain work experience (paid or unpaid) in an industry of interest. Interns are more likely to be given entry-level tasks but often have the chance to rub elbows with people in key positions within a company. In comparison to an apprenticeship, which offers very detailed training for a specific job, an internship offers a broader look at a particular kind of work environment.

Both are great ways to learn the ropes and stay one step ahead of the competition. Consider it dress rehearsal for the real thing!

Landes, Michael. *The Back Door Guide to Short Term Job Adventures: Internships, Extraordinary Experiences, Seasonal Jobs, Volunteering, Work Abroad.* Berkeley, Calif.: Ten Speed Press, 1997.

Oldman, Mark, and Samer Hamadeh. *America's Top Internships.* New York: Princeton Review, 1998.

————. *The Internship Bible.* New York: Princeton Review, 1998.

Peterson's Internships 1999: More Than 50,000 Opportunities to Get an Edge in Today's Competitive Job Market. Princeton, N.J.: Peterson's Guides, 1998.

Srinivasan, Kalpana. *The Yale Daily News Guide to Internships.* New York: Simon and Schuster, 1998.

NO-COLLEGE OCCUPATIONS

Some of you will be relieved to learn that a college degree is not the only route to a satisfying, well-paying career. Whew! If you'd rather skip some of the schooling and get down to work, here are some books you need to consult.

Abrams, Kathleen S. *Guide to Careers Without College.* Danbury, Conn.: Franklin Watts, 1995.

Corwen, Leonard. *Careers Without College.* New York: Simon and Schuster, 1995.

————. *College Not Required!: 100 Great Careers That Don't Require a College Degree.* New York: Macmillan, 1995.

Farr, J. Michael. *America's Top Jobs for People Without College Degrees.* Indianapolis: JIST, 1997.

Jakubiak, J. *Specialty Occupational Outlook: Trade and Technical.* Detroit: Gale Research, 1996.

Murphy, John. *Success Without a College Degree: The Secrets of How to Get Ahead and Show Them All.* Kent, Wash.: Achievement Dynamics, 1997.

Stoddard, Brooke C. *Careers Without College: Building.* Princeton, N.J.: Peterson's Guides, 1994.

Unger, Harlow G. *But What If I Don't Want to Go to College?: A Guide to Success through Alternative Education.* Rev. ed. New York: Facts On File, 1998.

INDEX

Page numbers in **boldface** indicate main articles. Page numbers in *italics* indicate photographs.